Praise for
Progressive Muslim Identities: Personal Stories from the U.S. and Canada

This anthology serves as a reminder that Islam, at its core, is a progressive faith that values justice and equality. With its unwavering support of the LGBT Muslim community, Muslims for Progressive Values is paving the path for a welcoming and inclusive Islam that values all of its followers, regardless of their sexual orientation or gender identity.

Faisal Alam, queer Muslim activist, speaker and writer
Founder of Al-Fatiha Foundation for LGBT Muslims

Progressive Muslim Identities: Personal Stories from the U.S. and Canada is the book we've been waiting for. For too long, Muslims have been defined as monolithically conservative on social justice issues like equality for those in the lesbian, gay, bisexual, and transgender communities. Muslims for Progressive Values (MPV) have refused to shy away from justice issues or from their faith. Not only have they stood with the LGBT community no matter the cost but they have taught us that it is not inconsistent with Islam to do so. This book promises to show the world the inescapable connection between belonging and equality.

Sharon Groves, Ph.D.,
Director, Religion and Faith Program Human Rights Campaign

Post 9/11 we have witnessed a plethora of literature from Muslim and non-Muslim scholars on the topic of Islam, women and Islam, Islamophobia, and extremism. However, this anthology is unique in its inception and goal; it adds an array of Muslim voices that have been buried by extreme and orthodox voices within Islam. This anthology relies on the mission of Muslims for Progressive Values, a non-profit organization that has created a space and a new horizon for Muslims of all kinds. This anthology brings back to life, and practice, an Islam rooted in the Qur'anic ideals of egalitarianism, self-determination, freedom of expression, human dignity and social justice.

Mehnaz M. Afridi, Ph.D., Assistant Professor of Islam and Director of Holocaust, Genocide and Interfaith Center, Manhattan College, N.Y.

This is a timely book, engaging and honest. A testimony to the universal human spirit that connects us all

Reza Aslan, author, professor, Middle East expert and Founder of Aslan Media, Inc.

The poetry of ordinary North American Muslims lives is not often recited, and is almost never anthologized. That is precisely why this volume is so important. It tells us the stories of Canadian and American Muslims in their own words. It also introduces us to Muslims for Progressive Values, and their work to create an Islamic space that simultaneously honours both Muslim and progressive values.

Amir Hussain, Ph.D., Professor of Theological Studies Loyola Marymount University, Los Angeles

This anthology of liberal and progressive voices is an important and heretofore missing thread in the complex and beautiful quilt of being Muslim in the modern world. The editors and contributors are thoughtful, honest, and courageous in sharing these stories. This book provides a touchstone for Muslims as we explore and examine our faith and for the world as it rediscovers the full face of Islam.

Saleemah Abdul-Ghafur Editor,
Living Islam Out Loud: American Muslim Women Speak

Progressive Muslim Identities
Personal Stories from the U.S. and Canada

edited by
Vanessa Karam, Olivia Samad, and Ani Zonneveld.

© 2011 by Muslims for Progressive Values

All rights reserved

Published in the United States by Oracle Releasing
8721 Santa Monica Blvd
Suite 141
West Hollywood, Ca 90069

Progressive Muslim Identities /
edited by Vanessa Karam, Olivia Samad, and Ani Zonneveld.

ISBN 978-0-9837-1610-5

1. Progressive Muslims. 2. American Muslims. 3. Canadian Muslims
4. Progressive Islam. 5. Muslims for Progressive Values. 6. Title.

Book design by E. J. Yarchk Hernandez

First Edition

Printed in the United States of America on acid-free paper

Foreword

Here is a collection of voices from the North American Muslim experience. The stories and essays in this book represent a myriad of Muslim voices that are as diverse as America itself. In the ten years since September 11th, 2001, politicians, the media and even religious leaders in the West have tried to paint the Islamic faith and the Muslim experience with a singularity of thought and purpose and agenda when nothing could be further from the truth. This limited way of looking at Islam and the Muslim world is perhaps in part what is responsible for the chasm in understanding that exists between the West and the Muslim world today.

Some may say that I am not exactly the ideal person to be writing the foreword to this book, and they wouldn't be entirely wrong. In my life I have probably frequented more bars than mosques, but my Muslim experience is as simple as my mother blowing *azaan* into my ears every time I see her, or my grandfather teaching me how to read the Qur'an in Arabic when I was twelve years old. A skill I later used to convince casting directors to cast me in Arabic-speaking roles by reciting passages from the Qur'an. Hey, I booked the job and said my afternoon prayers all in one go; what can I say.

What this book does so well is present a collage of Muslim faces and voices that allows all of us, Muslim and non-Muslim, to see a piece of ourselves. The only way to break the cycle of intolerance, misinformation, and prejudice is to connect to the human experience, to find the thing that binds us all. Whether you are religious or not, the stories and experiences in this collection will speak to you. For some they will resonate personally, for others they will be challenging, and for others they will offer a window into a world that you have not seen before.

Aasif Mandvi

A Note to the Reader

Within the pages of this anthology, you will encounter progressive Muslim voices you may not have heard before. The purpose of this anthology is to advance the conversation between progressive Muslims and the readers of this book by sharing what is personally meaningful in the authors' lives. Through this alchemy, we can each react to those ideas and see what is meaningful in ours.

These stories do not detail Islamic history or theology, or define terms you may have heard in the news. The authors' views are theirs alone, and not necessarily those of the editorial team or of Muslims for Progressive Values. As editors, because differences of opinion and even errors of fact are beside the point of the personal narratives of this text, we have focused our attention on the telling of the story. We have worked so that these authors can speak to you in their most authentic voices, whether that includes words in Albanian, Arabic, Chinese, or Urdu.

Therefore, as you read, you may also encounter unfamiliar foreign words and acronyms. For your convenience, all italicized foreign words are in the glossary, as well as some words that are not italicized, such as acronyms and the words "Allah" and "Qur'an." Because this is not an academic work, we have refrained from using a particular standard of transliteration in favor of letting regional pronunciations—the many flavors of the Islamic world—shine through. For this reason, you may find multiple spellings of the same word in our glossary. At times, we have used the spelling that best shows local pronunciation or the spelling preference of the individual author.

Because progressive values, human dignity, and freedom from oppression are important to us, we wanted to hear from other faithful Muslims who strive to live out these values. Thank you for participating with us in this process. We hope you will find, as we have, that it has been worth the effort.

TABLE OF CONTENTS

Introduction 1

The Emperor is Naked:
The Barely Coherent Ramblings of a Born-Again Buslim 5
  By Sahira Traband

Addio, Roma! 23
  By Jack Fertig

The Secret of Success 33
  By Jack Fertig

From Good Muslim to Best Self 35
  By M. Ameerah Saleem

Daughter of Shame 45
  By Olivia Samad

Los Angeles Convention Center 47
  By Olivia Samad

Amen, Amin 49
  By Sumaya Cole

Finding My Religion 61
  By Patricia Dunn

Living Up To My Name 67
  By Daayiee Abdullah

The Photovoice Project: An Interview with Rab Razzak 77
  By Ani Zonneveld

To Sink or Swim 85
  By Yarehk Hernandez

The Accidental Fundamentalist 95
  By Ameena Meer

Regarding the Imp Dancing on the Lintel 105
  By Dizery Salim

The Me Monologues 115
    By Mona Eltahawy

My Teacher 119
    By Ismail Butera

Allah Loves Us All 129
    By Shahla Khan Salter

The War on the Home Front: Queer Muslim Family after 9/11 . . 137
    By Tynan Power

Islam at Needle Point 145
    By Nakia Jackson

My Story: An Interview with El-Farouk Khaki 149
    By Afdhere Jama

Questioning the Answers 167
    By Ahmed Morsy

    Acknowledgments 181

    Contributors 183

    Fact Sheet – Muslims for Progressive Values (MPV) 189

    Glossary 193

Introduction

In the fall of 2010, I got a call from a Muslim friend in New York whose eleven-year-old son was assaulted by a schoolmate while riding the bus. The attacker was influenced by the prejudice around him and had watched comedian Jeff Dunham's and his puppet "Achmed the Dead Terrorist." My friend filed an official complaint with the school district at the urging of her Jewish friend, a lawyer. He told her that at a neighboring school district, kids had painted "Muslim go home" on a student's car. He also pointed out that it was only a few decades ago when Jews were "the Other." My own thirteen-year old daughter was taunted and called "terrorist" by her schoolmates in Los Angeles. These incidents made me realize that I had to act– this anthology is the result.

After 9/11, I not only came out of the closet as a Muslim, but fell into activism. As a songwriter and producer, I had kept my Muslim identity private for a long time. A lot of it had to do with my own insecurities as someone trying hard to fit into the entertainment industry. Keeping different aspects of my identities compartmentalized didn't feel honest. When one identity was lived out, the other parts of me felt suffocated. Blending all my identities together freely was transformational. Incorporating Islam into my music was my "coming home" moment. I produced an Islamic pop album. Instead of appreciation for creating a new genre, Muslim retailers and organizations told me repeatedly that what I did was religiously forbidden. According to them, music is only permissible if a percussion accompanies the voice, and only a man's voice at that! I was born and raised Muslim, and had never heard this interpretation of Islam. Fortunately, Ahmed Nassef, who was leading a new progressive movement, appreciated my modern pop approach. He introduced me to activism, and Patricia Dunn and Jawad Ali, the website editors of *Muslim Wakeup!*, introduced me to progressive Muslim writings.

Muslims for Progressive Values (MPV) is a non-profit organization I co-founded with Pamela Taylor in 2007 with chapters and affiliates in Los Angeles, New York, Washington D.C., Atlanta, and Ottawa, Canada. In our prayer spaces, families may pray together (like we do in Mecca), women may lead coed congregations, and mixed faith couples and LGBTQ Muslims are welcomed. For more information about MPV, please turn to our fact page.

Like Muslims in general, our progressive Muslim community is diverse, as is reflected in this collection of writings. We are African American, Caucasian, South and South-East Asian, Arab, Latino, straight, gay and transgender. Despite our wide diversity, what draws us all together is the common belief that Islam is inherently progressive, inclusive and egalitarian, an understanding that informs the principles of MPV. In this anthology, we don't claim to speak on behalf of all Muslims, but as a community, we want to share our values and perspectives in the public square.

This is not a book of Islamic theology or history; a reader looking for that has other sources. This book is a snapshot that captures the brave faces of individual progressive Muslims at this point in time. Their personal and honest narratives give readers a look into the lives of progressive Muslims in the United States and Canada. For the most part, the contributors are not professional writers or "famous Muslims." They are the voices you never get to hear.

Patricia Dunn finds truths in Islam that confirm her strong feminist ideals. Sahira Traband and Ameerah Saleem describe how their quest for authenticity brought them in contact with other religions and led them to a fuller understanding of Islam. We see in the writings of Dizery Salim and Nakia Jackson, two women who shed their conservative upbringing and struggle with being "Muslim enough." Olivia Samad's poems succinctly illustrate how conservative cultural and religious norms weigh on women inside even the most loving of families and continue to relegate women to the back of the mosque.

In an interview that highlights the Islamic call to help the oppressed, Dr. Rab Razzak talks to us about his experiences mentoring young black men in Los Angeles. And Ismail Butera shares the story of a remarkable teacher, an Albanian *imam* whose faith exemplified tolerance, humility, and compassion. In his interview with Afdhere Jama, El-Farouk Khaki reveals how he became an advocate for refugees escaping persecution for their gender/sexual orientation, and shares his moving stories of love, loss, family, and community.

Tynan Power writes about raising his children and facing layers of discrimination from the straight Muslim and non-Muslim gay communities. Jack Fertig describes how he converted to Islam in a gay-friendly space, despite the homophobia in the larger Muslim community. And Daayiee Abdullah recounts a personal journey that started from his discovery of Islam in China to his vocation as the only gay *imam* in America.

Mona Eltahawy's piece shows that conservative Muslim women and their Christian counterparts have very similar views on matters of sexuality. Mixed-faith marriages are another difficult topic our authors address. While a Muslim *man* marrying a Jewish or Christian woman is acceptable in the mainstream Muslim world, tremendous tensions arise when a Muslim *woman* marries a Christian or Jewish man.[1] Ahmed Morsy and Sumaya Cole talk about their mixed-faith marriages. Ahmed, an immigrant from Egypt, found common cultural connections with his Jewish wife and discovered his place in the world by questioning the answers he was given as a youth and as a sales manager in the rat race in New York. Sumaya candidly shares how her interfaith marriage challenged both the Muslims in her family and the Christians in her husband's family.

In their contributions, Shahla Khan Salter and Yarehk Hernandez both touch on the *Wahhabi* and *Salafi* undercurrents that have swept through communities in Canada and the United States. Shahla calls out the ultra-conservative *Wahhabi* sea of change that destroyed the tolerant and inclusive Winnipeg mosque her father helped build. Yarehk's initial brush with *Salafis* demonstrates the breadth of beliefs that fall under Islam and shows both why the extreme interpretation can be compelling and why it was not sustainable. Ameena Meer shares her assessment of the Islamophobia storm, giving us a first-hand look at the many issues and assumptions surrounding the Park51 Islamic Center in New York City.

As we approach the tenth anniversary of 9/11, it is our job to make meaning out of this national tragedy. Muslims must continue to demand that progressives and liberals within the Muslim community are represented in our public discourse. While many non-Muslims have stood in solidarity with their

---

[1] None of the established *imams* and religious heads will marry such a couple. MPV is proud of our work in providing officiant services to all loving adult couples.

fellow Muslim citizens, 22% of Americans say they would not want a Muslim as a neighbor, 44% say Muslims are too extreme in their religious views, over 50% of Americans believe U.S. Muslims are not loyal to the United States,[2] and 39% support a requirement for Muslims to carry a special ID.[3] Muslims have been demonized for political convenience to secure more votes. In Canada, 55% of non-Muslims don't believe their Muslim compatriots share their values.[4] Shortly before publication of this book, the Southern Poverty Law Center released an intelligence report detailing a concerted and aggressive activist campaign of Islamophobia in America that seeks to "build a widespread, irrational fear and hostility against Islam in general."[5]

According to a Time Magazine Poll conducted in August 2010, 62% of respondents say they don't personally know a Muslim American. But, what the mainstream media paints as the typical Muslim is not the majority of us. Our men do not all wear beards and robes and our women do not all wear veils. This anthology tells us the stories of many authors who may not appear Muslim according to the prevalent stereotypes. Their religion and spirituality, and the way they live out their Islamic faith, is quietly interwoven into their daily lives. It is very likely that you have met many Muslims like us before. We are your neighbors and colleagues. And maybe, through the stories presented here, you will see yourself in us.

Ani Zonneveld

---

[2] Esposito, John L. and Mogahed, Dalia. *What a Billion Muslims Really Think*. Gallup Press, 2008.
[3] Gallup Poll: July 2006.
[4] Léger Marketing, September 2010.
[5] Steinback, Roger. *Jihad Against Islam*. Southern Poverty Law Center Intelligence Report, Summer 2011, issue no. 142. http://www.splcenter.org/get-informed/intelligence-report/browse-all-issues/2011/summer/jihad-against-islam.

The Emperor is Naked:
The Barely Coherent Ramblings of a Born-Again Buslim

By Sahira Traband

I am a self-identified progressive Muslim; nevertheless I felt unqualified for inclusion in this anthology. Although it is not a popular position, I am quite certain of and completely at peace with the progressive part of my identity. As the feminist adage goes, the personal is political, and my progressive convictions emerged directly from my life experiences. The Muslim part, however, is ridden with internal conflict, paradox and continuing challenges. In addition, low self-esteem and egomania conspired, so that I resisted writing this essay with all the self-destructive powers at my disposal, (and they are a multitude). Finally, sitting before the twenty-inch Hewlett Packard altar, praying for humility and inspiration, I realized that all I could offer is this story of my life. Hopefully it is enough.

In 1969, when I was three years old, my family and I left our cosmopolitan town in England for my father's village in central Pakistan. The contrast between Cambridge and Muzzaffargarh was total; both brutal and amazing. We brought the first car and the first white woman, and they were equal in their novelty. My blond-haired, blue-eyed mother, years before her current *hijab* obsession, refused to practice *purdah*. She remained resolute despite the entire clan's horror; she certainly didn't wear a *burkah* over her mini dresses when she went out in public back home, and she bravely refused to be a hypocrite just because she had relocated. But television wasn't to intrude on Muzzaffargarh for some years yet, so white skin was truly fascinating, and after being pawed relentlessly every time she left the family compound, my mother quickly found the benefits of borrowing her *bhabhis'* black veils.

My little sister and I arrived with our hair ribbons matching our dresses, smelling of rose bushes and rain. We brought with us our dolls with their ribbons and dresses, beds and tea sets. And there, amid my family's relative opulence, contrasted with my toys' outrageous affluence, for the first time I encountered people who lacked food and clothing and shelter. Whenever we left the high walls of our compound, we were met with the swarms of hungry, naked children that claim and coat the landscape as rightfully and plentifully as the dust and the flies. They begged for *pesas*, and we learned the correct response to make them retreat. I thought, "*Maaf kurro*," meant, "Go away," since leaving was the dejected response of those wretched souls. It was many years and many visits later that I learned the true meaning of this mantra was, "Forgive me." Whether or not they forgave me I do not know, but I was never able, nor can I still, forgive myself.

It was clear to me then, and has always remained so, that it was wrong for inanimate objects to have more than suffering people. Long before I knew the theory, before I had even the language to describe it, this primary experience shaped me irrevocably and completely, maybe more than anything else that has ever happened to me. From this moment, my progressive politics were born, upon this axiom were built all my other beliefs, and against this position all others have been tested. The questions I need answered are questions of justice, and everything reduces to that. Progressive politics responds in a voice which is fair, and I have always felt comfortable answering its call. Nothing that has happened since has disproved or diminished my conviction in the morality of progressive principles. I am a socialist and a feminist, and my children's godparents are lesbians. I have protested wars and organized sit-ins, and though I voted for Barack Obama, he is a compromise far to the right of where I stand.

When I was young, older people would enrage me with their patronizing forecast that I would outgrow my radical ways. But I am the older people now, and I can safely assert that age and experience have not disproved a fad and relieved me of my progressive beliefs. Over the years I have definitely mellowed in the ways I express myself. I don't debate politics at the dinner table and no longer assault men who make inappropriate sexual remarks. I tell the jokes that once I deplored, and can tolerate with only minimal judgment the kind-hearted bigots that I love. But nevertheless, I am as left-wing as they come and have not once fluctuated in or questioned my political principles.

Sadly, not so when it comes to calling myself Muslim. After all these years, it's the Muslim part of my identity that still lacks conviction. And it is not because I am some self-hating Muslim, an Islamophobe, as they call them these days. I don't think Islam is any more damaging to the human spirit or world peace than any other religion.

Although I was born into a Muslim family, for over half my life I made no claim to Islam whatsoever. When I was eighteen, I was rejected by my ultra-conservative family because I wasn't good enough. One of my uncles is an *imam*. He has memorized the entire Qur'an, and he cleans his teeth with a twig rather than toothpaste because he thinks that makes him a better man. Although I now call myself Muslim again, I remain a hesitant and faltering follower at best. Using my uncle's criteria, armed with my Toms of Maine, I am no kind of Muslim at all.

The Dalai Lama says, "There is no need for temples; no need for complicated philosophy. Our own brain, our own heart is our temple; the philosophy is kindness." While I check the Muslim box, I find more solace in the Tao Te Ching than the Qur'an, and deserve the Buslim moniker a friend has jokingly, but accurately appointed me. I like my drawers and closets organized but prefer a little anarchy in my spiritual life.

When my English mother married my Pakistani father she converted to Islam, but neither of them was remotely concerned with religion in those early days of their brave and scandalous love. They were too busy defending themselves against their outraged parents and trying to find an apartment that would rent to a mixed couple.

I was the oldest child, born in London in 1966. My sister was born two years later. My memories of our early childhood are sadness dipped in magic. Secrecy and fantasy and hope and despair comprised the potion. We had a garden full of flowers and apple trees, pet rabbits, and a shed at the end where the fairies lived. Life was idyllic in between the beatings, and I swore to marry my sister when we grew up so our family would always be together. We were Muslim because we got gold bracelets on *Eid*, but we celebrated Christmas with a fabulous white and silver tree (it was the late 60s, and metal was mod) and we learned the Lord's Prayer at school.

Twice during my childhood we drove 6,000 miles, through ten countries from England to Pakistan. We took ferries across the sea and drove through clouds in the Alps. I ogled pornography at a German border stop and saw gypsies dancing in countries that exist no more. I stood on a bridge with one foot in Europe and one in Asia. Our car got stuck in mud at the Turkish border, Mount Ararat gazing down indifferently in the distance. I got lost in a Tehran bazaar. When we were stopping in the Khyber Pass, a man put a shotgun through my dad's window and asked for cigarettes. Fortunately, he was a smoker. The topography and language and currency changed constantly. I changed permanently.

The best part of my childhood was when we lived in Pakistan. Gone were the stifling conventions of suburban English life in an isolated nuclear family. On our family's compound I had nearly total freedom. I saw little of my parents and loved it that way. We roamed in a tribe of cousins, moving from one family home to another at will, being fed and chastised and comforted by whichever auntie was presiding. We played house, cooking stiff *chapattis* over fires on flat roofs at sunset. Unnoticed, we slipped out to the bazaar to buy sweets, and held tight to teenage cousins on moonlit motorcycle rides to the desert. We chased goats. We had an Arabic tutor who was hired to teach us to read the Qur'an, but no one took the unfortunate young man seriously, and we children spent most of our time tormenting him. We slept ten in a bed and somehow managed never to get the lice my mother was sure we would contract by such unsanitary, un-English practices. Five times each day, the sweet sound of the *adhan* spun out into the ether from the little neighborhood mosque. It was this call to prayer, not a clock, that measured our days. (Even now, it is the incorrect Urdu pronunciation I prefer to any Arabic perfection.) We loved to heed the call, running through the alleys to get to the mosque in time to pray. Outside was a common water pump where we washed and splashed. Inside was cool and quiet. We huddled together in a little clump, praying what words we knew. It was a short dream, but a happy one.

When I was nine years old my family emigrated to the United States of America. I couldn't wait to go, because like the rest of the world I had a vision of the promised land. I wanted to visit Disneyland, live in a penthouse apartment, and have a swimming pool in my backyard. On a cold November night we arrived at JFK airport. The four of us moved in with my father's cousin's family in a one-bedroom apartment in Flatbush, Brooklyn. *Amreekah* was a shocking disappointment; there wasn't a palm tree or swimming pool in sight. They were hard times for us, classic immigrant times. My parents were ill prepared for the difficulty of finding work in a recession or staying warm in a New York winter. With only my mother able to find a job, my parents could afford boots for the children only. We were taught to sneak beneath the subway turnstiles to save money on the fares. I remember trying to return a penny to my father intended for a piece of Bazooka bubble gum so he could have enough to pay the rent. We learned what cockroaches were. My mother was hospitalized with a nervous breakdown.

Added to the instability, the poverty, and the lack of a national, ethnic, or religious identity, was the particular suffering created by the emotional and physical abuse that plagued our family. We took that with us wherever we went. I don't want to imply that I experienced the most abusive childhood ever. That would be disrespectful to those who have suffered far worse injury than I. Indeed, my own parents' childhoods were far more traumatic than mine, and I remain grateful (and amazed) that they succeeded in not passing on some parts of their legacy of abuse. But both of them were beaten by their parents, and they used violence and fear to control me for seventeen years.

My mother projected her toxic shame onto me and hopelessly attempted to exorcise her demons by making me into the perfect daughter. She demanded total obedience, and I constantly failed to meet her unrealistic expectations. Any independent expressions that were out of line with her rigid standards threatened my mother's need for control. No aspect of my being was beyond the realm of her judgment, and, like all self-righteous people, she established herself as God, and her warped version of reality prevailed. While my sister chose a different path, I was not a compliant child and defied my mother constantly. I did not drink the Kool-Aid and recognized as much of the truth as my sanity could tolerate; I proclaimed to anyone who cared to listen that the emperor had no clothes.

My father was simply not present for most of my childhood. When he wasn't at work, he cloistered himself in the basement or garage. He was disinterested at best, but for the most part he shunned me. My clearest memories of him growing up are when my mother called him in for reinforcement during my beatings. That was when I became really afraid. I wore glasses from the time I was six, and my greatest fear was that he would accidentally smash them into my brain and kill me. Once my father got going, even my mother got scared. The session usually ended with her begging him to stop.

Most damaging of all was the message that I was unlovable. I was told over and over that only my family knew what I was truly like because they lived with me. Everyone else was fooled, but when they got to know me like my family did, they too would see what a monster I was. The argument was circular, but completely convincing to me then. I am forty-four years old and still struggle beneath its incontrovertible weight.

After searching on three continents for the right place to settle, my parents finally came to rest in suburban New Jersey. They found a town so provincial that I spent my adolescence responding to questions like, "Where is Poggstown?" when explaining that I was from a country next to India. When I was fourteen and my sister was twelve, my parents succeeded in having the son they had always wanted. Three years later, they repeated their triumph and another son was born. Photos were sent to Pakistan of my brothers naked, displaying their penises for the trophies that they were. The minimal time and attention that I had received from my parents was further diminished. I was relegated to the role of unpaid nanny and housekeeper. A new and better nuclear family was born, and my sister and I had become irrelevant.

Conservative Islam was taking root amid the growing population of Muslim immigrants in America. My parents quickly gravitated to this fundamentalist interpretation of Islam, appropriating it to justify their rigid control over their daughters. Though we were not forced to wear *hijab*, due to the conservative Islamic dress code, school sports, public pools, and days at the beach were no more. My mother took our school photos off the walls because any depiction of the human form was considered idolatrous. My father took his smoking to the garage. Christmas evaporated, and, like the dresses my mother used to wear and the beer my father used to drink, it was never mentioned again. We practiced Islam as a duty rather than a celebration. I was subjected to weekly Islamic Sunday school where we wasted our time throwing spit-balls and gossiping in the stairwells.

I completed reading the Qur'an in Arabic, fulfilling an obligation and understanding not a word. I fasted every *Ramadan*, floating around in the above-ground pool in our backyard with my sister and my best friend, trying not to swallow water or let the neighborhood boys gain a glance at our forbidden legs. Faith was a burden rather than a balm. I would torture myself by reading passages in the Qur'an describing the damned boiling in hell for all eternity. Although I tried to be good and pray as many times a day as I could, I knew I was a sinner and could never be good enough. I prayed to be transformed into a rabbit because I knew animals didn't go to hell. I was traumatized by guilt and shame.

In school we did not date or go to parties or dances. Jewelry and make-up and anything that made us attractive were discouraged. I did not violate these tenets behind my parents' backs because even if they weren't watching, God was, and I believed. Despite my sometimes paralyzing fear, I loved God very much. I can remember often crying with love for God while saying my prayers. Somehow the specter to whom I prayed the obligatory prayers and the Spirit with which I communed voluntarily were unrelated.

Although a few close friends at school knew I was Muslim, most people did not. Because I resembled my mother, my skin, especially in those New Jersey winters, was light. My parents had changed my name when I was six months old from Sahira to Sarah, and Sarah gave nothing away. I internalized the racism and Islamophobia and passed as white and Christian. I lied about Christmas presents that I never received, and on the few occasions when my dark-skinned dad came to school, I made sure not to walk too closely beside him through the hallways. As I grew older I began to have difficulty reconciling my personal experiences with my religious teaching. Among my best friends were twin sisters who were Unitarians and atheists. The dilemma for me was that these "infidels" were the most ethical people I knew. How could these good people be the sinners, while so many believers in our Muslim community lacked any semblance of integrity, honesty, or compassion?

At seventeen, I started college, of course still living at home, with a schedule of my classes posted on the fridge. I met a boy who made vain promises, but I was so vulnerable, so needing to be loved that I believed. He was six years older than I and had lost his own religion somewhere between high school and a master's in philosophy. He lied to me about many things, but about one thing he told the truth: He cautioned me that I would not be able to continue on my path of questioning and seeking and still remain a Muslim. The relationship lasted only a few miserable months, but despite my commitment to proving him wrong, within a year I was Muslim no more.

After failing General Biology, dashing any last hope of becoming the doctor that was the de facto expectation, I settled on sociology as my major and philosophy as my minor. And as my faith deteriorated, I was in agreement with Dostoevsky's Grand Inquisitor, wondering how a god can expect us to believe in him without sending us a Jesus every generation. It was asking too much. If God didn't send me a Jesus real quick, things were not going to go well. I took women's studies classes, and my rage gained a direction and a name. Until that point my feminism was intuitive. Now I had back-up and was ravenous for the theory and herstory I was consuming. I became politically active in numerous leftist causes and questioned the validity of fighting for the rights of oppressed people when, as a woman, I myself was oppressed by my family and culture. In the Islam I was taught to believe in, asking questions was heresy. For the first time, I met openly gay people and I was unable and unwilling to condemn them because judgment and discrimination are the sins, not loving. My faith further unraveled.

Meanwhile, our conservative Muslim community was rife with examples of hypocrisy and compromise, sheep who gobbled all the privileges of membership within the fold while violating every principle that same community supposedly valued. One of the pillars of our community, the head of cardiology at a prestigious hospital, had a fleet of Mercedes which bore vanity license plates emblazoned with his eight-year-old son's name, followed by "MD." While safely ensconced in this Muslim household, my sister and I were taken by that same son on a surreptitious but proud tour of the good Muslim doctor's extensive collection of porn. Wealth was next to and just above godliness. Collusion with the illusion was the expectation, but the enticements were meager, and the emperor still looked naked to me.

In the mid-1980s South African apartheid was in its death throes. Hastening the end, university leftists forged a coalition movement to place economic pressure on de Klerk's regime by demanding that their schools divest money from companies doing business with the South African government. On April 12, 1985, I helped plan and execute the take-over of our college student center for a protest planned to last until our demands were met. My parents were not racists; they were proud of me and had videotaped me on the evening news, lying down in the street. That night when I came home to pick up my sleeping bag and toothbrush so I could return to the sit-in, reality collided rudely with my lofty ideals.

My parents forbade me to return. There were boys and drinking there. It was out of the question. I argued that by taking part in the sit-in, I was being a good Muslim since Islam condemns racism. I claimed all sorts of moral high ground, but my appeal fell on deaf ears. In truth, it wasn't saving the world that was motivating me the most. I was leaving to save myself. My mother physically refused to let me go until I dragged us both to the phone and called the police. Then she threatened to commit suicide if I left. My father told me if I left I could never come back again. They let me take nothing because they said nothing was mine. I walked out the front door and my sister threw down a sleeping bag from a bedroom window. Fundamentalist Islam had just claimed Cat Stevens and I launched into the wild, wild world.

My mother didn't kill herself. My father drove to the sit-in to give me his permission after all. I promised them—and meant it—that when the protest ended, I would come home. The students predicted that our victory was at hand, but the university was tenacious. It was thirty-seven long, glorious days before they capitulated under public pressure and media exposure.

We slept outside on the concrete, in the cold and sometimes rain. I had never been happier. I had a boyfriend, sort of, who was a revolutionary, or at least looked the part. With his bourgeois West Indian background masked by proletariat posturing and a beard and khakis, it was central casting at its best. His accent helped me overlook his narcissism. There were hunger strikers. I met Jesse Jackson and I heard Bob Marley for the first time and felt him in my soul. I tasted revolution and alcohol and sex and freedom. It was an intoxicating brew. I knew I was damning myself to hell, but I had this one chance to enjoy life, and my plan was to return after the sit-in ended and repent for my remaining days. I was sinning on credit, paying the steepest of interest, and I gladly accepted the terms.

I remember the guilt I felt at hoping our demands would never be met so that I could keep my borrowed freedom forever. But after thirty-seven days the university divested and our triumph was celebrated in a hail of happiness.

I was bereft. I said goodbye to my new friends, my lover, my brief bliss. I returned home, fully expecting life to go on as normal. But as the poet wisely wrote, "I can never step in the same Alan Ginsberg twice."

I was dying in my family and I knew it. When I prayed nightly for forgiveness for being the wretch that I was, I puzzled that it seemed my parents were the ones who brought out the worst in me. I could never be a good person, the person God and I wanted me to be, when they were near. By the grace of God I sensed that spiritual development was impossible in their midst. The lure of the would-be revolutionary was the perfect transitional object, the ideal comfort and distraction. Five weeks later I left again.

If I had known how hard it would be, I would never have had the courage. I had forty dollars, no job, no home, no support, and no refuge. I was denied access to my siblings, had my health insurance cancelled, was deprived of my education, cursed and called a whore. My mother came only once to see me, because after that she said where I lived didn't exist. My father threatened to shoot and kill me for the shame I was causing my family. I was abandoned by my extended family on both sides and the entire Muslim community with which I had grown up. Because my parents had tied my relationship with them to my relationship with Islam, I lost my religion too. When I hear people talk about the hardest thing they've ever done, I know mine was leaving home.

The world was wild, but somehow I survived. (Cat Stevens fading to Gloria Gaynor?) Gorging on freedom that tasted sweeter than anything I could have imagined, there were many times when I choked. Innocent teenage girls raised in strict Muslim homes who suddenly have complete and total freedom don't always make the safest of choices. I wasn't allowed to use words like "drunk" and "pregnant" growing up. Three months after leaving home, I was both.

These were years of immense sadness and suffering, only partially numbed by the copious self-medicating. I loved my family and grieved for them. My little brothers were more like sons to me and their loss felt nearly unbearable. I was poor, sometimes too poor to afford food although I always had cigarettes. Life was unstable, risky, and dangerous, and suicide was always Plan B. But I was too afraid to actively take my own life. I didn't believe in guns, couldn't afford pills, and after reading about a woman who committed suicide by freezing to death, I tried to go outside into the February New Jersey night but gave up because I got too cold. I scraped razors across my wrists but that looked like it was really going to hurt. Most of the time I settled for alcohol poisoning and unsafe sex. At least parts of that were fun.

I did not renounce Islam in a poetic gesture as I walked out of my parents' door. But rather over some time, in clumsy lurches like a large, sinking ship. My mother had spoken on behalf of God for years, and I could not distinguish between their voices. They had appropriated Islam and taught me that God was on their side, so He couldn't be on mine. Angered at what I perceived was a rejection by Islam, I struck back. Still partially believing in the horrors of hell, I defied eternal damnation and rebelled in the extreme, rejecting not just Islam, but God Himself. I scorned all religions and scoffed at the delusions of believers. I attempted atheism, which was the ultimate sin, yet ironically felt more honest and whole and good than I ever had before. Losing God did not make me immoral: I did not tell more lies, litter, or change my behavior in any way. Instead, gone was the hypocrisy; I was purged of doubt and contradiction and had total integrity at last. It was an uncomplicated pause, a necessary resting place, but not, for me, the answer.

When I was nineteen I went into New York City to see an esteemed psychic. She saw an elephant crushing my spiritual chakra. If I wanted to survive she advised that I stop suppressing my spirituality. I still don't know if I believe in psychics, but I believed in her message. I realized I couldn't remain an atheist, but I couldn't revert to Islam either. Instead, I learned that there was a third option. I could be spiritual without being Muslim; I could have God without religion. Eventually the elephant moved on.

So much was wrong, but I didn't know how to make it right. Harkening back to my gypsy childhood, I decided the problem was location. I packed my books in a friend's attic and left America with a one-way ticket to London. From there I embarked on a hitchhiking tour of Europe. In an ashram turned youth hostel in Amsterdam, staying up all night smoking hash and debating existential questions, I first encountered Buddhism.

Oddly my problems followed me and my geographic cure did not work. I returned to America, the Trinidadian and the craziness. It was all getting old. I was twenty now and my self-destructive tendencies were killing me. Everyone in my world was self-medicating. We used drugs and alcohol to celebrate, to mourn and to cope. I never met a drug I didn't like. They all altered my reality and blunted the pain. They stopped me from following through on my suicidal impulses, preserving me as they killed me incrementally.

I moved to yet another shabby room for rent, this time in a crack house. One night, shortly after moving, I was alone in my room unpacking, when a loud, clear voice spoke out, asking me to make a decision. It was asking me to choose life or death. I responded aloud, asking for more time to think it through, but I knew time was running out. There was no further dialogue. The whole exchange lasted only fifteen seconds, and as soon as it was over I dropped to my knees on the filthy carpet, grabbed my always-nearby journal and wrote it all down so I would never forget. Well, I've never re-read that entry, but I've never needed to. I haven't told many people about that night, maybe two or three in all these years, but I have never forgotten it. I was relatively sober, so it wasn't a mushroom- or LSD-induced hallucination. And though there were no burning bushes, trumpets, or fanfare, a voice outside me posed a question, and I was alone in that room.

Perhaps there are some people who can smoke crack socially, but I would not have been one of them. The next day I shared the story with my sister and she came to get me. For her wise intervention I am grateful. The stint at home lasted only a few days. Despite all the enticements of upper-middle class comfort that my family had managed to attain, the restrictions that were stifling before were impossible to tolerate now. As much as the separation from my siblings tortured me, the choices were extreme: having my family or my sanity, but not both. When there are only two choices, and one of them is sanity, there is really no choice after all.

I stumbled and fell into a supportive, spiritual self-help community, and they caught me just before I hit the floor. I stopped self-medicating. Without the numbing effects of all my favorite distractions, the pain crashed in. I began for the first time in my life to learn healthy coping mechanisms. I learned to lean on God. I didn't have much God back then, but the support group taught me ways to cultivate that relationship. They told me it didn't matter who or what my God was, just as long as it wasn't me. With the help of the motley crews who assembled nightly for their own survival, I found my way forward.

It was obvious that I was a case for seasoned professionals. I started formal counseling and began years of dredging the pond scum. The horrible, dark stuff of our past. The shame and guilt and fear oozing along the bottom that, if not brought up to the surface, will eventually contaminate the water completely. It would be cool if there were another way. If we could swim in the sunlight without stirring up the mud. But unfortunately all the short cuts I've discovered so far have dead ends.

I nourished myself on books about spiritual and emotional development. I made friends who showered me with unconditional love. (It's hard to imagine a loving God if you don't know what real love feels like.) I learned about healing circles, tried massage therapy, spent three years doing breath work, and chanted affirmations. I tried all kinds of yoga, attended the services of various progressive religious congregations, went on retreats, and did group therapy. I lay in isolation tanks, attended more support groups, and prayed in every conceivable position. As lost as I was, attracting all the craziness I exuded, I continued to encounter teachers and truths who, one at a time, built the road that would lead me out.

It took me six years to get a bachelor's degree. Work and meetings took priority over classes. After I graduated, I became a teacher in an inner-city high school. It was the best job I have ever had. In those grim, gritty classrooms, with no heat in the winter, no books, sometimes not even a curriculum, I learned far more than I ever taught my students. It was more social work than teaching, because it is hard to make history relevant to a boy who is hungry or a girl who is pregnant. I taught classes in French (and I speak very poor French) because it was the common denominator between me and the Haitian immigrants who were literally washing up on our shores. My coworkers were a largely dejected, dispirited lot, not there by choice; one of the security guards was a pimp. Daily I journeyed to that city that was closer to Muzzaffargarh than the comfortable place I lived only ten miles away, and I cannot count the times I cried all the way home. I was continually asked why I worked under such unpleasant, even dangerous conditions. The answer is that I received the greatest tribute of my life in those classrooms. No certificate or medal could trump the precious gifts of respect and trust and love I received from those who had been betrayed and suffered much in their brutal world. I was awed by my students' glorious strength; their hope despite their suffering humbled me.

)90, I came out as bisexual. It was a different time than it is now, and my administration threatened to fire me if I told my students. Thanks to the intervention of the American Civil Liberties Union, I was the second public school teacher in New Jersey to come out of the closet. I discovered a queer South Asian support group, and for the first time since leaving home had Muslim friends and spoke Urdu and ate home-cooked curry. I was amazed at how they still loved Islam, prayed *namaz*, and celebrated *Eid*. They felt no need to renounce their religion due to some differences of opinion on relatively minor points. Even when they had been rejected by their parents, they did not feel rejected by Islam. Still, I did not believe Islam could be for me.

When I was thirty-one, I met my husband. Fred and I have the opposite of every love story ever told. Our energy combined and we combusted in a beautiful shower of shooting stars, thereafter quickly descending into darkness. We each brought our own dysfunctions, and the concoction was toxic. Intense, inexplicable attraction kept us together until our first child was born; only then did we both love something enough to do the growing that was needed to be happy together.

Fred loves me. He knows all my secrets, has watched me wander in my shadows; I have wounded him, frightened, disrespected and tried to control him. Still he loves me. He is the first person I have ever believed might actually stay. I read a lot of fairy stories as a little girl, and it has not been all happily ever after. We have had our struggles, more than some and less than others, but we have been able to spin our straw into gold. I am so grateful to be living a happy ending.

When my sons were born they gave me blood family again. When you have lost every person to whom you are related, that is a precious thing. Parenting our children in a non-violent, humanistic way has been immensely healing. The most difficult and most wonderful thing that has ever happened to either of us. It's so good that I still expect to wake up and find out it was all a dream. In the middle of the night, when I'm having very bad thoughts, my happiness feels undeserved, stolen, and I am sure I will have to give it back. As it turns out, I did not become a doctor or an ambassador for the United Nations as I had once dreamed. But although so many of my life's goals fell by the wayside, having a happy family has happened after all.

After twenty years in exile, for reasons she has never explained, my mother enlisted a people-finding service and contacted me. Reconnecting with my family has been a mixed blessing. They have changed a little, but I have changed a lot. The 3,000 miles between us is not always enough. Despite all the work, I still want to have had a different past and a better family.

I did not initially call myself Muslim again, but over time I discovered there are many interpretations of Islam. I read about Mansur al-Hallaj, a ninth-century Sufi master, who would fall into trances in which the complete obliteration of his ego allowed him union with the Divine. In a state of ecstasy he exclaimed, "I am the Truth," the Truth being one of the ninety-nine names of God. For his heresy, Mansur was executed. His words were so threatening that they cut him into pieces and burned his remains. I had never learned about Mansur growing up. We didn't study Muslims like him. If Mansur could achieve such communion with God on the path of Islam, then I wanted to walk on his road.

With an open mind but fear in my heart, I started exploring the religion into which I had been born, but from a perspective far different than the one with which I had been raised. I couldn't believe how much there was that had been concealed from me. I couldn't believe how distorted the Islam was that I had been taught. How small, how stunted, how crippled and limited. There was a long, glorious history filled with music, art, mysticism, and most importantly for me, social justice. I discovered a philosophy of peace, that *jihad* meant struggle with one's inner demons, that mercy and forgiveness were stressed above all. I finally read the Qur'an in English. Nowhere did I unearth a proscription for dressing the way my mother advocated, but I was amazed at how repetitive was the commandment to adopt orphans. I was stunned at the real focus of the religion being about kindness and justice for the disenfranchised, community, reverence for truth over hypocrisy, and the belief in the one God of us all. This was not the Islam I had been taught. This was an Islam I could love, an Islam worth striving for. It turned out that those beliefs I held most sacred, the ones for which I had lost so much, were actually the very ones that the religion of my birth most valued. I began to reincorporate Islam into my identity and my life. I experienced reconciliation in the deepest recesses of my soul.

Several years ago, my husband made a decision to convert to Islam. Fred's focus is not on such details as praying five times a day, but he makes contact with his higher power on a pretty constant basis. He works hard to be the best husband, father, son, and friend that he can be, and in twelve years I have never witnessed him deny money to a homeless man. Fred is comfortable with his faith. While he works hard on himself, he does not agonize over the questions that still keep me up at night. He keeps it simple. Sometimes I am very jealous.

We decided to raise our sons, Teo and Mikail, with a Muslim identity. Only time will tell if they will be thankful for the exposure or need an extra therapy session somewhere down the road. Loving community, I embarked on a mission to find a Muslim congregation. We tried a number of mosques and Muslim groups, but none met our needs. At most of them, our family had to be separated in the gender-segregated spaces, but it is hard to develop your family's spiritual bond when you can't be together at spiritual gatherings. At other gatherings, the focus seemed to be more about displaying material accomplishment. Everywhere our Muslimness was questioned and we never felt comfortable.

Just as I was ready to abandon the search for community and accept that we would practice as best we could alone, I discovered our progressive Muslim group. The first gathering we attended was like finding the mothership, like coming home. My poor family were gun-shy after several years of being dragged to yet another Muslim group where the men wouldn't shake the women's hands and we got chastised for entering through the wrong door. But here there were mixed-gender groups of people laughing, with hands extended readily, and hugs soon to follow. Everyone was welcome, no questions asked. You were Muslim if you said you were Muslim, and if you weren't Muslim at all, that was just fine too. Anne Lamott writes of her beloved church, "It's where, when you show up, they have to let you in." That's what our group does for me.

I'm still not much of a Muslim by my uncle's definition, though I try not to use that dictionary anymore. Nevertheless, I love Christmas more than Eid. (Who wouldn't prefer a holiday spent singing songs and decorating a tree over one whose most visible expression is the slaughtering and butchering of livestock?) I've abandoned all but communal prayer in Arabic, preferring to talk with God strictly in English, the only language I know well enough for begging, raging, and loving. Not modesty but vanity lurks behind my reluctance to don a bikini, and the only thing that covers my head is a beanie when I'm cold. I'm still struggling with the details. For instance, I like the name Divine, for God, but I admit it sounds more like a brand of fancy chocolates than the deity I try to believe in and know. My God isn't sweet and calm and lovely, my God is violent and powerful and ecstatic, like giving birth and making sublime love and the monsoons in my father's village. God is everything, and not everything is divine; some things are profane but they are God just the same.

I remain suspicious of the religious. I practice irreverence. I am bad, and commit things. I have been a black sheep for so long that I like it. I make sure to dye my roots if any white wool creeps in. In fact, the closer to God I come the more I rely on sacrilege to keep me grounded. I balk at being religious because it smells so similar to self-righteousness, so much like the scent of my mother. Maybe I still don't feel worthy of being Muslim. Like the servants in Pakistan who squatted in the corner, always ready to spring up and serve, never part of the feast, part of me still doesn't feel entitled to sit at the table. But I wonder, "What would Muhammad do?" and I stand up to take my place.

Part of the reason why I stay is a stubborn refusal to yield to the zealots. As my friend Yarehk, a Latino Sufi, says, "Don't give way to cultural imperialism; this is our Islam!" I don't want brave Mansur to have suffered in vain. Those Sufi mystics who ceaselessly sought and sacrificed all for Truth deserve attempted emulation, no matter how shabby. And I have never stopped loving the sound of the *adhan*, no matter how far from the mosque I have traveled. How wonderful it is to once again heed its call. (There's a reason it graces every movie soundtrack that can possibly justify its inclusion.) And maybe I stay because when I am faced by something hard or scary, I catch myself uttering the prayer *Bismillah* without thinking. It's just what I do, because it's who I am. It is comforting to have one's roots and branches on the same tree.

There is a *hadith* where God says, "Take one step towards Me, I will take ten steps towards you. Walk towards Me, I will run towards you." In my still-unfolding story, I am sometimes limping, sometimes leaping, but always moving, along.

Addio, Roma!

By Jack Fertig

"Are you a Muslim?" a handsome young man from West Africa asked.

"No," I answered. A voice in the back of my head added, "Not yet." That question and both answers, the expressed and the unexpressed, were getting very familiar.

The young man smiled and told me, "Yes, you are. Anyone who comes in peace is a muslim." As he said that, it occurred to me that there are capital-M Muslims, who have said the declaration of faith, probably grew up in the religion, but could yet be usurers, pimps, or warmongers; and there were small-m muslims, who lived humbly and charitably, whatever their faith or lack thereof. Of course it was the same with Christians and christians. The voice in my head got a little louder. "Not yet."

It was in June of 2003, and I had just arrived in Toronto for a joint conference of Salaam Canada and Al-Fatiha, the Muslim GLBT organizations for Canada and the United States, respectively. I had been reading about how feminists and queer folks fared in the Islamic world and had developed contacts and conversations on the Internet. I wanted to attend this conference to hear these topics addressed personally, to meet some of the people I'd been chatting with online and reading about, and to flesh out the questions I'd been exploring over the last two years.

Up to that point my exploration of Islam had been strictly academic. I had been happy as a Roman Catholic. It was a spiritual home I had worked hard to find a place in, and I had no plans to leave it. Like many progressive Catholics, I understood the people of faith to be the Body of Christ and the old men in the Vatican to be a necessary inconvenience. (As I was learning about Islam, there was no such body of old men. Once you declare your faith it cannot be questioned. Your own personal relationship with God is unmediated and cannot be judged by anyone else. Well, that's the theory. As in all religions and ideologies there is a bit of difference between the ideal and the practice.)

Religion has always been a matter of personal exploration for me. My parents were agnostic. Both grandfathers had rejected their strict religious upbringings (one Catholic, one orthodox Jewish), and my grandmothers came from observing, but much less strict homes. Except for a year at a Unitarian church, the only family involvement with religion came with my parents' divorce, when my father decided his children would be Jewish. I enjoyed Hebrew school and religious education, but after a while it felt more like he was using this as a wedge against our gentile mother.

On top of the long and horrible history of anti-Semitism that every Jewish parent teaches his or her children, there were the stories handed down about the medievalist nonsense, rituals, and attitudes that both my grandfathers grew up with and rejected firmly. My agnostic Jewish grandpa recalled with annoyance the prayers and restrictions he had to contend with as an orthodox Jew in Silesia. He preferred to talk of the time he glued a sleeping rabbi's beard to the table. My other granddad never would have dared such a stunt. His mother, a painfully upright Catholic woman, regularly threatened hell and damnation for much less. On the other hand, in my family's deep involvement with the Civil Rights movement in the 1950s and 1960s, and then the anti-war movement, we went to many church events and met countless clergy and laypeople whose religion was key to their commitment to social justice. For every Torquemada there was a Berrigan Brother; for every Father Coughlin a Martin Luther King or a Dorothy Day. Religion was clearly a powerful tool, and you could make of it what you would.

As an out gay teenager in the early seventies, laws and logistics kept me away from bars and meetings of the Gay Liberation Front, but I started going to the Metropolitan Community Church, a "non-denominational church for all people" created as a welcoming spiritual home for GLBT people. I found good company there, decided to read the Gospels, and was eventually baptized. Later in college I met some Wiccans and studied witchcraft. A few years later my first husband, a gorgeous Brazilian named Luiz, taught me about the Brazilian macumba tradition that syncretized West African gods with Catholic saints, reconciling two seemingly contradictory sets of belief. Much of what I gained from these religious explorations helped to create my stage persona of "Sister Boom Boom" a Christo-pagan priestess-cum-drag-nun in the Sisters of

Perpetual Indulgence, an order of "Gay male nuns dedicated to the expiation of stigmatic guilt and the promulgation of universal joy."

"Perpetual Indulgence" lived up to its name—well, in my case anyway. Many bad habits were well in place before I started wearing one. The Sisters do a lot of good, but for me, with all the benefits we hosted for Cuban refugees, for the Gay Olympics (while we could still call it that), and for AIDS organizations just as they were starting out, I was rarely without a joint and a glass of booze. Emceeing many of these events was a glamorous masquerade that largely camouflaged and accelerated the disorder in my life.

After about five years under the wimple and make-up, I felt lost and hollow behind a flashy façade. I ended up in treatment for addiction and alcoholism. There I learned that alcoholism and addiction are spiritual diseases. Organized religion was not particularly recommended, but in my own prayers and meditations I found that to be where I needed to go.

The Episcopal Church seemed a comfortable fit for my Catholic yearnings and independent mind, but after a bit of joking about it as "Catholicism lite" (all of the same great smells, yells, and bells without the heavy guilt and dogma!), I reconsidered. The Episcopal Church deserves better than being treated as a lite back-up, and frankly, I don't do lite. I never cared for lite beers, white bread or milk chocolate. Like my food and my men, I like my religion complex and with dark undertones. It was clear that the Roman Church, with all the S & M of Saints and Martyrs, and Symbols and Mysteries, and the liberationist communities struggling with the Magisterium, was where I belonged. With a year of training and discernment, it was indeed a good fit for many years, and for whatever criticisms I may have had of Pope John Paul II, Cardinal Ratzinger, and Opus Dei. I was in good company, admiring of Pax Christi, the Catholic Workers, and the work of liberation theologians.

I went back to school to get a bachelor's degree in history and spent a year studying in Florence, an excellent base for travels during class breaks. In February of 2001, a week in Istanbul brought me face to face with the Islamic world—as a tourist, not a seeker. No, that's not quite true. I'm always seeking to learn, and Istanbul introduced me to entirely new perspectives, a crossroads of cultures with the wealth of a once-great empire built on the experience of previous Middle Eastern empires.

Besides the historical treasure trove that it held in store, Istanbul reminded me of how little Americans know of the contemporary Middle East. Already tensions were high. Al-Qaeda had bombed the garage of the World Trade Center, President Clinton had bombed an aspirin factory in Sudan, American meddling in the Middle East was already causing serious problems. It was clear that misunderstanding and prejudice were having far too much effect on American politics and policy development. Americans needed to be better informed, and there was only one American I could be sure of educating.

My spring semester was already set, but for the next year I signed up for a series of classes on "The History of Muslim Societies." To supplement the academic, I also got in touch with GLBT Muslims online, learning about feminist activism in Muslim countries and pursuing information that was not available on the TV news. Six weeks of summer classes in Morocco immersed me in a Muslim culture—in many ways more considerate, polite, and cooperative than society in America—and the experience of life in a post-colonial nation.

Having since spent time in a variety of Muslim nations I can easily answer the oft-put question: Would I want to live in one? Let's reframe the question. Would I want to live in a country that was struggling from colonialism or war, or still trying to pull a democracy out from under a military elite that might take power when dissatisfied? No. One thing that became very clear in my travels in Dar-al-Islam and from watching the news from an economic/historical perspective, is that with very few exceptions "Islamic nations" are neo-colonial client states under dictatorial rule backed by the United States, the United Kingdom, and/or France. Our government talks a lot about promoting human rights in the Islamic world, but watch where the money goes! In Morocco, money was clearly going to those who already had plenty. The lingering problems of colonialism were vast, but in all classes and situations I encountered *adab*, the Islamic culture of courtesy, whose simple gentleness and respect for all impressed me deeply.

The more I learned about Islam the more attractive it became. There is no compulsion in religion; nobody may judge another's faith. God is all mercy and all compassion. In fact the most repeated phrase in Islam, *Bismillah irrahman irrahim*, identifies God as All-Mercy and All-Compassion. All people are created of equal value in the eyes of God and none may intermediate between any person and God. Of course these points are central to all the Abrahamic faiths, but they seemed so much more articulated and affirmed in Islam.

Back in the States, classes in Islamic history revealed its intellectual depths, the neo-Platonic arguments, the science and philosophy of the medieval period. But if Islam produced such genius then, why is the Islamic intellectual world in such a dismal state today? Again, economics. Any great center of learning is first a center of wealth. It takes money to fund research and learning. Wherever you see great universities and intellectual progress, there is a culture of wealth to support it. Not that wealth guarantees learning. When Spain and Portugal were rich with new world loot they missed their opportunities. So did the Ottoman Empire. But money makes it possible. Even far-off Timbuktu was able to develop as a center of education because it was a wealthy trading post.

Further reading revealed a historic acceptance of sexual diversity and even some pederastic traditions much like those of the earlier Greeks. Taking a pretty teenager under my wing is not my thing, but in earlier centuries there was no shyness about acknowledging and accepting same-sex love. While the great Arab poet, Abu Nawas, is often condemned for his "wicked" love of boys, his homoerotic poetry has never been without an audience. A number of Islamic cultures also had roles for people we would now call transgender. In Pakistan there are still *hijras*, transwomen, who serve various roles in folk culture, singing and dancing to bless weddings and newborn babies. Alas, they do not have the respect these days that they used to.

Wahhabist innovation and colonialism have imposed a very strict sexual ethos in most of the Muslim world, much at odds with the stories of Sheherazade, belly dancers, or the sexual adventures of Sir Richard Burton. Before we got the modern notion of the puritanical Islamic world, the Middle East was portrayed as a land of lavish erotic decadence. Both views are Orientalist stereotypes, but digging deeper I found richer, more nuanced and accepting Islamic views of sexuality than what prevails today. Even before beginning an earnest search into the world of Islam, I'd read that the first published use of the word "sodomite" to suggest homosexuality was in a medieval Spanish tract against an Andalusian caliph. It seemed that the Muslims took for granted pleasures that shocked good Christian folk.

There had also been a Gambian classmate, a woman with a mass of beaded braids cascading to her shoulders. She always wore mini-skirts and looked so young in them I was surprised to learn she was in her mid-forties. That she was a Muslim was less surprising. "Of course I want to go on the *hajj*," she told me, "but then I'll have to cover myself all the time with long robes and a headscarf. I'm not ready for that yet."

Islam, I would learn, was a "universal religion" not because everyone is to adhere to a monoculture, but because it is a basic set of principles, clear and simple. My Gambian classmate was only one example. Cultural practices among Moroccans, Turks, and Muslims I met in the States were extremely diverse. There is a solid, unyielding core in the five pillars of faith—the declaration of faith, prayer, fasting, charity, and the pilgrimage—but this core can fit into any culture and allows for a very full range of human diversity. The Qur'an even says that God created us differently so that we may learn from each other.

OK, so there's so much more to Islam than I'd suspected, and it could be a comfortable spiritual home for me. In fact, the more I learned about Islam the more it appealed to me. The principles struck me as very simple and clear, but building into very elegant ideas of respect for nature, individual dignity, and human rights. The five daily prayers and other small consistent reminders of our relationship to God brought forth a mindfulness that seemed rare in the West.

But I was quite happy where I was, and for me one of the great points of Catholicism was the incarnation—the belief that God lived as a human to affirm the inherent human link to the divine. In the Islamic view, Jesus Christ is a prophet born of a virgin. His conception is described as a divinely-ordained parthenogenesis, but without any father, mortal or divine; God has no begotten son. The human race is no more of the family of God than any of the other animals of His creation. Rather humans need religion because we stray from our true nature. Animals, on the other hand, don't.

Planning my trip to the conference to Toronto, this occurred to me as I reflected on the thought that the Christian notion of humanity being above the animals and closer to God has been much abused, offering free rein to despoil the earth. This notion began to feel like a very anthropocentric view of creation. Islam's affirmation that humans need religion and animals don't puts our special relationship with God in a different frame of reference. Our more highly developed brains need spiritual focus to balance our intellectual hubris. Also, a principal purpose of spiritual work in any religion is to be more present in the moment, to be more accepting, and to let go of things we don't need, in other words, to be more like an animal. With these ideas I was able to let go of the Incarnation, to accept that I could embrace an Islamic view of Jesus. This felt very significant and it felt as if there were no reason I couldn't be a Muslim. But that didn't mean I should be one.

At the conference in Toronto, I was able to meet and talk with writers and activists, to attend lectures that confirmed and supplemented my own research, to meet new friends and to meet face-to-face a few I'd chatted with online. I felt very much at home with my new friends and felt that much as I was welcomed as an ally of the community, I could gladly become one of the community.

I prayed with Muslims, making proper *rakat* for the first time, following the example in front of me. My first attempt at Islamic prayer was led by a woman, with men and women praying together. As we were nearly all queer, praying behind someone of a different gender would less likely be a distraction than the usual arrangement. The prayer was simple, beautiful, direct. It felt very right and natural, and I would join with the community, sharing in their prayers through the weekend. We were all praying to the same God, and although there were some phrases I could not repeat in good faith (or could I?), I had worshipped many times with others not of my own faith, sharing as much as we could.

Saturday I attended a Sufi *dhikr*. A handsome young man dressed all in white lit some candles, led a chant, and continued chanting while spinning in the middle of the room. At one point we were all invited to participate as the spirit moved us. I stood and felt swept away, laughing, crying, spinning, open to God, spiritually naked, accepting, and free, as if I were dancing with the Universe. The community had welcomed me and now I felt as if God were welcoming me.

Yes I could join this community, but should I? I was far from home, enjoying the company of a very particular group. I'd seen enough of the Islamic world to know that I would not normally be praying with other GLBT people in an air of open gender-equality. Any mosque at home, any mosque anywhere would be much more traditional and conservative. It would be prudent to go home and think carefully about converting before actually doing so.

Another *dhikr* on Sunday was much less ecstatic. The leader taught us simple steps and chants that we would do in the prescribed fashion. The first two chants were simple expressions acknowledging divinity, love, and similar reflections. The third one was much more memorable. *La illaha ill Allah wa Muhammad rasul Allah.* There is no god but God and Mohammed is His prophet. It was the declaration of faith. Could I say it? And considering the importance of that declaration, did I dare? As I turned the question over in my mind I realized something very important. In our circle at that *dhikr* was David, a Jewish volunteer there to translate for a deaf attendee, very much a friend of the community, but he excused himself from this third dance. He could not say the *shahadah*, and everyone present respected that. It forced the question for me. I asked the leader, "If I were to say this, would it make me a Muslim?" I knew the answer, but had to be sure. She responded, "If you say it and mean it, yes, it could." Of course there is no god but God. I knew that from childhood reciting *Shema Yisrael Adonai Eloheinu, Adonai echad* (Hear, O Israel, the Lord our God, the Lord is one), and even with the convolutions of the Trinity, Catholics are monotheistic. And as I had just realized, yes, I did believe that Mohammed was a prophet of God.

I also realized that were I to wait sensibly to make *shahadah* at a mosque in San Francisco, I would probably never have the chance to become a Muslim while singing and dancing with gay men and women.

I learned the dance.

I sang the words.

On Sunday, June 20, 2003, I became a Muslim.

As if it were a necessary part of my initiation, I was held up by an American border agent on my way back into America. First time that ever happened! Because I was Muslim? He could have no way of knowing. It was a slow day and he just wanted to look at all the pretty stamps in my passport, to ask me about the ones he didn't understand. After explaining the one-year student visa in Italy and the Yugoslav stamp in Cyrillic letters, I was getting a bit nervous about the Moroccan stamps, all in Arabic. Of course he had to go all the way through and get to those! He nodded as I explained my summer of classes in Fez. Then he remarked, "Morocco isn't a good place for Americans to go!" Never get into a needless argument with a border agent, but I just had to ask: where should Americans go? He thought about it for half a second, said, "Hawai'i. Hawai'i is a good place to go," and waved me through.

I haven't been to Hawai'i yet (someday, *Insha'Allah*), but I have since been to Iran, Bosnia, and Malaysia. In Iran I prayed at the Imam Reza Shrine in Mashhad, a space that felt as vast as St. Peter's in the Vatican, but with a simpler decor. St. Peter's is filled with an eclectic collection of statues, paintings, and sarcophagi calling attention to a variety of saints and patrons of the Church. The tiles in the Imam Reza Shrine spell out Qur'anic *ayat*, or represent stylized designs of flowers and stars, all calling attention to the word and the works of God, simple elements in a complex design. Sitting in contemplation with hundreds of other people in a large courtyard, I felt a deep sense of serenity, a perfect state of harmony in a divinely created universe from stars to flowers, all pulled together with the words of God.

The Secret of Success

By Jack Fertig

(*To the tune of "When I was a Lad" from "H.M.S. Pinafore," by Gilbert & Sullivan*)

I looked for a way to build my fame
And make sure that the world would know my name
My efforts all were failures and I must confess
I haven't any genius and my talent's less
(Ev'rything I tried at was an awful mess!)
But irritating the Islamic community
I'll make myself a millionaire celebrity!

Now, Rushdie I will grant you is a brilliant man
And all the furor set off wasn't in his plan,
But when he got his fatwa and was forced to hide
His sales were astronomically multiplied
(His sales and recognition reached the sky worldwide)
And when the Ayatollah cried out for his head
Sir Salman hid beneath a very comfy bed.

When Ayaan Hirsi Ali lied to join the Dutch
She found that lying more could lead to very much
She lied about her background and her family
And then declared that Islam's just misogyny.
(She swore that Muslim women never could be free)
And now she's sitting very pretty in New York
With magnums of champagne and fancy cuts of pork.

A bodice ripper hacked out by Ms. Sherry Jones
Relates the life of A'isha in breathless tones
Professor Spellberg called the research weak
And suggested it could put some Muslims in a pique
(This made the unknown writer the star of the week!)
And now the blogosphere is roiling angrily
For one hack writer symbolizing all that's free.

The formula for fame is really very clear
I'm writing 'bout the prophet as a drunken queer
And when my book's rejected as a load of piss
I'll blame my failure on the fear of terrorists.
(Fox News will have me on and boost my sales for this!)
And even though my writing is a lying mess
I'll be declared a hero of the open press.

From Good Muslim to Best Self

By M. Ameerah Saleem

I always found having a connection to a higher power gratifying and remember wanting to be a good Muslim as a young girl. My idea of a good Muslim was simply following traditional Islamic principles and rituals as practiced in the community I belonged to. I was raised within a structured Muslim environment where we made *salat* five times a day, covered our hair, and wore modest clothing whenever we stepped outside of the house. I could not wear sleeveless shirts or short skirts unless pants were worn underneath. I could not wear fitted pants unless I wore a loose, long shirt on top of them.

Growing up under these rules, I saw that our religion required members to be disciplined and could be quite strict in terms of women's dress. These practices, however, never interfered with being engaged in everyday life outside of our home. My mother saw to it that I was exposed to social activities, extracurricular opportunities, and summer vacations. We supported our non-Muslim family's church events and often ate dinner with them during the Thanksgiving and Christmas holidays. For the majority of my childhood and adolescent years, I believed that the scarf I wore on my head and my loose clothing served as proof of what a good Muslim I was. I saw these as outward statements of faith.

The earliest part of my education was through Muslim and Afro-centric schools. The environments here were very similar to the one I was used to at home. I received further instruction in Qur'anic recitation, Islamic studies, and African-American history. When I transitioned into the public school setting, I became uncomfortable with being around non-Muslims outside of my family, as there was a constant focus on differences in our dress. I wore a scarf to cover my hair and pants underneath my uniform dress; these outward statements of faith became an issue. The students teased me and often overlooked our similarities because of how I outwardly identified myself. I thought it was silly and scary how quickly someone could decide and believe you aren't acceptable to them over religious differences. I was only trying to be a good Muslim, not to appear as though I was anti-non-Muslim. Eventually, they saw that I was not as foreign as I appeared to be.

As I continued my education in the public schools, my friendships with non-Muslims blossomed. My closest friends in high school included Baptists, Pentecostalists, and African Methodist Episcopalians.

I joined the Eastern Senior High School choir during my sophomore year. At that time, I was the only Muslim in a group of Christian singers. I continued to wear my scarf and agreed to wear black ones during our performances to match with everyone else. I attended church services with many of the choir members, and they would also visit the *masjid* for *jumaah* when it was possible. We traveled around the city, singing a repertoire of jazz, blues, Christmas carols, spirituals, and gospel music.

One day, while watching a choir documentary, the director asked me if I ever felt swayed or conflicted singing and listening to gospel music. I told her that I know what I believe in. My participation was not out of a need to live a double life; I just enjoyed the experience of singing and the opportunities it afforded such as learning how to harmonize, read music, and travel with my friends. My appreciation for gospel music also comes from growing up around a family of choir singers. Many of the youth in my Muslim community were also involved in the arts and we supported each other's events. We never questioned each other's sincerity to Islam, and I never felt that we weren't good Muslims as a result of this participation.

When I left for Spelman College, I joined the Muslim Student Association (MSA) immediately and was excited to have a support network of Muslim youth already in place. We would go to Friday prayer together, the movies, have potlucks at each other's homes, and host events with MSAs in the surrounding area.

Once, an MSA friend accused me of participating in *shirk* for singing in my high school choir. She was a fan of a prominent hip-hop artist. I mentioned that some of the hip-hop music we blindly support can be vulgar or degrading, but that gospel was uplifting and inspiring more often than not. In retrospect, her criticism discouraged me from joining our college glee club because most importantly, I wanted to be seen as a good Muslim. Subconsciously, I felt I was under scrutiny and began to spend less time with the MSA.

I formed relationships among the greater student body, as I wanted my friends to reflect more than only one aspect of myself. I felt that my non-Muslim friends accepted me as-is and supported my self-development.

My college experience served as a sort of rebirth for me. I was introduced to courses on feminism, which I initially thought was about angry, rebellious, chauvinistic women. I read a required text and concluded that I had feminist beliefs even though I had never identified as one. I am a feminist because of my concern for the well-being of young girls and women, my belief in equal rights for humanity, my advocacy for my own livelihood. Feminism is about being the sole owner of my choices as a woman, regardless of the expectations from men, as well as, other women.

I began to question my place within Islam at this time. How can I be feminist and Muslim? Isn't that a paradox? Why don't Muslims—especially in America—confront the poor treatment of women in the United States and abroad? Where are these questions coming from? What happened to the good Muslim girl in me? Who am I becoming? I mostly reviewed texts on Black feminism, as these were more readily available. To a certain extent, I also assumed information on feminism in Islam was limited.

I began to redefine my idea of a good Muslim, which became more about being my best self. Instead of comparing myself to others in general, I wanted to practice self-actualization and measure myself against my own standards. I transformed according to what I cared about instead of how others may have wanted to see me. In my junior year, I grew out my relaxer of over ten years and locked my hair. This was my statement of resisting mainstream ideals of beauty and the extent I had previously gone to attain it. I wanted to accept the state of my hair as it grew out of my head instead of obsessively straightening it with chemicals or a pressing comb every two weeks.

During the transition, I stopped wearing my scarf as I began to feel that I was wearing a scarf only to be seen as a good Muslim by other Muslims. I didn't see not covering as wanting to show my hair or become a Rastafarian. I wanted to embrace my new consciousness and profess a statement. What I wanted to show was that faith and modesty live in the heart. You can see them in a person's character, not in her head-wrap. I wanted to fracture the assumption that the more colorful your scarf or elegantly wrapped it is, the more likely you are to be a better *Muslimah*. I was breaking through my own illusions of what a good Muslim woman is supposed to look and think like. As uncomfortable as this process was, it was very freeing.

After graduating from Spelman, I moved to New York City. It took a while for me to seek a Muslim community to connect with, as I wanted to further avoid experiencing the kind of scrutiny I had in college. I stumbled upon a social group of Muslim women and hoped to find solace, thinking that perhaps they were also going through the same thing. One time I posed the question why it is considered unacceptable to not wear *hijab* and be in a natural state of beauty, yet acceptable to wear our scarves as a large colorful display and be in an enhanced state of beauty? A simple discussion became an argument and was quickly ended by the group leader, who deemed it *fitna*. I felt misunderstood and estranged for having my thoughts, but I never looked back after that. I figured out how to be alone without being lonely and found solace within. I never wanted to disassociate with being a Muslim, but I was quite progressive by comparison to this group and former classmates in the MSA and often felt as though I didn't belong.

I decided to enroll in the Institute for Integrative Nutrition, which exposed me to different philosophies on health—physical, mental, spiritual, and financial. A common saying at the school was: "It's one thing to live and another to thrive." I had never considered the importance of emotional health and its connection to spiritual, physical, and financial health until then. I felt stressed by the City and deeply frustrated and confused over why the traditional Islam I was raised to practice was not working for *me*. I kept trying to jam myself into this box even though I was unable to find the inspiration that I had been lacking. I spent a lot more time questioning but not understanding what I was experiencing.

I began journaling as a form of therapy and started writing poetry again. I needed to find answers to my own questions and decided to start from scratch. If Islam is a natural way of life, then it preceded this religious context. I mapped out my beliefs, dissecting and deconstructing everything I was taught to believe. I redefined Allah by removing the idea that God is and can only be male. I came to the conclusion that the Creator is neither male nor female, as those are physical characteristics that the Creator transcends. I stopped referring to the Creator exclusively as "He." I believe we were created in the spiritual image of the Divine, not the physical image. Throughout history, patriarchal societies have considered the female as unholy and unworthy. Male is usually the preferred sex, the more righteous of the two. Male is believed to validate female. Referring to the Creator as "She" is even blasphemous and simply ridiculous to many people today. However, I believe that if we can classify the Creator as male, then we can classify the Creator as female. I believe the Creator is neither exclusively male nor exclusively female, but balanced like yin and yang.

I moved away from needing an intermediary to validate my connection with Allah, realizing this higher power is also within me. The same energy that exists above and outside of us also resides within us. I stopped victimizing myself for believing differently and not accepting concepts in traditional Islam that didn't fit my understanding. Another saying at the Institute was: "Feel the fear and do it anyway."

I took the advice, as I felt it was critical to being my best self. In a journal entry, entitled "for sale," I wrote:

>anybody got change for three years of fear???
>i got five rolls of duct tape
>nails and hammers
>and a stack of wood planks
>left over from trying to keep out the sunshine
>guess i found delight in being blind,
>wasted so much time.
>can i get fifteen cents for a cup of regret?
>ok, fine let me get a dime
>i need something to burn while i make my bets
>planning and promising that
>imma get it straight, get it together
>things will be better the year after next.
>may as well get rid of this procrastination too
>i'd give it to you for a penny
>but i never really put it to any use

> except for once when i couldnt find my groove
> and another time when i couldnt escape
> cause i didnt have any running shoes
> what did i ever do to be so black and blue?
> listen to me trying to find another excuse
> better yet, take everything - it's on me
> if i hold on to this shit i'll never feel free
> all i need to do is keep trying to improve
> praying consistently and paying my dues
> what else do i really have to lose?

I learned valuable lessons in self-awareness, faithfulness and perseverance at just the right time. I left New York to move back to Atlanta. My mother passed away not long afterwards. I couldn't imagine this happening in the midst of the emotional instability I experienced while living in the City. To cope with her passing, I started vocalizing my feelings and continued with journaling and writing. I introduced myself to meditation and visualization techniques and practiced yoga more regularly. I read about the chakras, which are energy centers of the body, and strengthened mine through daily meditation. I noticed overlapping beliefs across cultures and religions, despite our differences in practices. I found empowerment and inspiration on this path, in contrast to the conflict I felt in traditional Islam. This is how I imagined it felt to be my best self and Muslim.

For my birthday, I took a trip to Los Angeles and immediately fell in love with the health-conscious lifestyle and the sense of open-mindedness. The city had an energy that was missing in New York and Atlanta. I was determined to make Los Angeles my new home. Within two months, I had found a job and relocated.

A few months after moving, I discovered the Bodhi Tree bookstore, which exposed me to an even greater wealth of spiritual information that validated my new practice of faith. I spent hours reading books about spiritual journeys from diverse standpoints and cultures that were somehow similar to mine. I vowed to believe outside of the box from that point forward, but I still continued to attend *jumaah* on Fridays at traditional *masjids*.

Each time I attended service, I revisited issues of gender inequality. The *masjid* I attended for almost a year had men and women separated by a short partition with blinds stretching across. One day I came in after missing a few weeks and the sisters' area had been turned into a room where we now had to listen to the *khutbah* on a small-screen TV. No one seemed to protest or even care. I then vowed to maintain my own spiritual space and not to expect others to be in charge of my belief system.

I came to define a Muslim as one who submits their total will to One God. In my opinion, submitting your will to a higher power means being open to the unknown, to shifts and changes and having faith through it all. It means being flexible, adaptable, and seeking conscientiousness and understanding instead of passing judgment. This One God is the Creator of many cultures, and therefore many paths are available to connect with Allah. I feel that traditional Muslims engage in inter-religious dialogue, but rarely entertain intra-religious dialogue. There are various cultural contributions to Islam, yet there seems to be a general consensus that we should only follow practices originating from the Middle East. Somehow, practices originating in Africa, Asia, and on other continents are rendered inferior. I don't believe that Islam requires us to drop our ethnicity and cultural traditions that are such a large part of our experiences or our ancestors' experiences.

My independent spiritual practice incorporates new age and metaphysical principles, gospel and inspirational music, and African, Native American and Buddhist teachings with Islamic ones. I have a strong appreciation for universal teachings and deeply connect with spiritual concepts and traditions that speak to Carl Jung's idea of a collective unconscious. For example, different cultures have similarities among the way they prepare and dress for prayer as well as the way prayer is performed (i.e. hand postures, kneeling, rhythmic recitation or chanting).

Throughout my spiritual journey, I remained open to connecting with the Muslim community but unwilling to compromise my spiritual values just for the sake of belonging. I wanted to build relationships with Muslims who cared about the same causes and were open-minded enough to discuss issues related to social justice within Islam and the larger community. One day, I came across the MPV Meetup group and decided to join. I was curious to see how progressive their values actually were and what kind of initiatives they were involved with.

Over time, I have shared information with the group on the similarities between postures in yoga and *salat* and they listened without jumping to conclusions or criticism. Progressive Muslim is a term one must define for oneself; however this group of Muslims reflects the overall idea of what I ultimately value on my spiritual path. MPV is the first group I've found where I can be honest about my concerns and be heard. As we say in MPV LA: "This is a place where you can be yourself and be Muslim."

Before being a part of this group, I wasn't in favor of marrying a non-Muslim nor accepting homosexual Muslims, mostly out of fear of not being a good Muslim and because traditional Islam justifies the discrimination of both. I no longer believe that marrying a non-Muslim nullifies my faith as a Muslim. I believe it is most important to build a union around similar values and characteristics. I find it unjust to persecute and/or take away the rights of people and to ban them from our brotherhood solely based upon their sexual orientation. I believe that if we are all born Muslim, then this not only includes heterosexuals, but also homosexuals. We have been conditioned to equate homosexuality with dysfunction, as though heterosexuality implies perfection.

My conversations with the group's co-founder helped me define what it means to be a Muslim with progressive values. Through MPV I feel a personal and shared sense of accountability to practice values of faithfulness, compassion, wisdom, and justice. We practice an all-inclusive faith; an Islam of equality and righteousness. In my opinion, this is essential to developing my best self and most importantly, to simply being Muslim. Some practices that work for me may not work for others in the group and vice versa. If we don't see eye-to-eye on an issue, we still respect one another's voices and opinions. Our sense of egalitarianism and humanitarianism is what inspires me about this community. It challenges me to part with outdated ways of thinking and existing within Islam and my personal life and to continue to examine my beliefs and grow as an individual progressive Muslim within our community and society at large.

I have learned that regardless of what community and environment I live in, I must have my own set of rules and codes of conduct to live by, separate from the mandates of the mainstream or dominant culture. My beliefs and values are conscious choices, not ideals I have adopted simply because they have been dictated to me.

Daughter of Shame

By Olivia Samad

You've come home.
In the house, decorating for your sister's wedding,
Unbidden, you make tea
for your guests and inlaws, expertly.

You are smart, you go to college, but you go so far away.
You are pretty and artistic, but in a too-thoughtful, brooding way.
You are young, full of promise,
but you won't listen to what the Imam says.

Do not dare to do or be anything
but what we have deemed right for you.
We believe, unquestioningly,
In a God that is small and full of blame.

We are your amma your baba
your imam your umma.
You are our beloved
daughter of shame.

Los Angeles Convention Center
By Olivia Samad

Why go to the mosque on this day
When I never go on others?
I go instead to the LA Convention Center
Where each year they have Eid prayer.

The Republicans and the Democrats have convened there.
Last weekend, it was the porn industry.
In the 11th grade, it was the state science fair
where I won first place in chemistry.

I pay $15 to park in the garage with curved concrete ramps and walls
and walk into the South Hall,
echoing with steps and sound,
White, like a blank page with no margins or lines,
Awash in light that can refract into everything.

Today, Americans reach back to traditions
that came with their families pre-emigration,
wearing djellabas and kaftans and the festive colors of jubilation
from Croatia, China, Ethiopia, Lebanon.

I meet the thirty others within this kaleidoscope of Muslims
who identify as progressive, who support marriage equality,
who wanted to pray together on this day at this public event.
The men in our group enter through their privileged entrance in the front.

The women sit in the back, where the words of important men —
the Imam, the Mayor — are overwhelmed by reverberation and the sounds of children,
Our distance from what matters blurs the sound of the speakers
in a buzzing that resembles anger.

Even in this secular space we are separate.
Last year, when a woman tried to find her husband,
A young man ran, as if for his life, to guard the men's area,
shouting, "Sister! You cannot go there."

Like the city it is in, it is a backlot.
This place, always becoming any story its occupants decide to tell.
Why not, one day, one of unity, harmony, and even, gender equality.
Like all things sacred,
It is large enough to contain even the profane.

Amen, Amin

By Sumaya Cole

"Bismillahi Rahmani Rahim"

"Father God, thank you for this food you've so graciously provided us with. Thank you for the roof over our heads and the clothes on our backs. I pray that this food be nourishment for our bodies and please bless the hands that prepared it. In Jesus' name I pray."

"Amen," "Amin"

I looked up Cassius' phone number in an old email and called him that evening. I had him meet me at our favorite Mexican spot in his neighborhood, asking him to bring me the things I had left at his apartment on the day we broke up. I didn't want him to suspect anything. I needed to see his reaction first-hand. Maybe that would help me decide whether or not I wanted him back in my life.

Cassius and I had fallen in love one and a half years ago when we were both working at a middle school together. I was a special education teacher, he was the dean of discipline; I was mixed, Congolese-Middle Eastern-White, he was African-American; I was Muslim, he was Christian. Struggling on and off with family expectations and our religious differences, we had finally decided to split up for good. We hadn't spoken in weeks.

I waited in the dark parking lot until he pulled up, and then I got in his car. I didn't want to meet him inside because then we'd have to commit to spending the whole meal together, and I had no idea how he was going to react to this, or if I wanted to stay to see it. I had practiced it over and over in my head: "I'm with child, Cassius," or, "I got knocked up," or, "We're having a baby!" I ended up sticking to the basic, "I'm pregnant." His face didn't move or flinch. I kept going: "I don't want to be together, and I can do this alone, no problem. I just wanted to tell you because I felt like it was the right thing to do. Don't feel like you have to do anything or be a part of my life or anything like that. I can do this alone. I definitely don't want to get back together."

He stopped me. "I didn't want to say anything because I was scared about what you were going to say, if you were planning to have an abortion or if you wanted me out of your life. I'm here." It was a short and inconclusive conversation, and we got out of the car to go into the restaurant. Over *camarones a la diabla* and *enchiladas*, we talked, and even laughed, about the situation. We decided not to get back together just because I was pregnant. But if this was real, we were going to raise a baby together, no matter what happened between the two of us.

On Friday morning, we went to the doctor together to take the official pregnancy test. My doctor was a middle-aged Arab woman, who, after lecturing me about being more careful with birth control, gave Cassius a piece of her mind. "You'd better be planning to make an honest woman out of her!" Inside I was laughing and cringing at the same time as she grilled him. I knew this was nothing compared to the wrath he would face from my family when they found out. I avoided telling them.

I hated to see my mom celebrate my losses, still hoping that I would find a Muslim husband. Unfortunately, my brother had let our mother know a week before that Cassius and I had broken up. Her knowledge of our break-up would only add fuel to the fire when we shared the news about my pregnancy. It was real now. We were having a baby. And I didn't have a bone of excitement in my body. This was not how I had imagined starting a family.

Cassius told his family about the pregnancy. They took it in stride and may have been disappointed, but didn't show it. Over the following weeks, I could feel his sister honing in on me with her Bible in one hand and a net in the other. I kept a safe distance, but took every opportunity I could to learn more about their faith.

I had joined their Bible study classes and constantly asked questions. I had difficulty understanding how they likened a man to God or even gave God human characteristics, which in my religion was *haram*, sinful. It was also hard for me to understand their strict and literal approach to a human-written text. Muslims believe Mohammed received the word of Allah, which was written down as the Qur'an. I couldn't understand how they knew that men wrote the Bible, but still interpreted it as a holy, all-knowing text. The Bible studies gave us an opportunity to debate these issues and understand each other's perspectives. We didn't always agree, but we did learn to respect each other's beliefs. Despite what seemed like glaring differences, our values were the same. We were both believers with a mutual respect and love for each other, and a different path to God.

Not everyone thought that engaging as we were with each other's religions was good for us. When Cassius told his pastor about the pregnancy, the pastor's reaction was a shock to me. He told Cassius in confidence that he would have to leave me. He had to concentrate on his religion and beliefs, and not let this situation, or me, distract him. I was appalled. I couldn't believe that a religious leader would say something like that. When I finally felt comfortable going to see his pastor, we decided to go together. I explained to him that I had no intention of steering Cassius away from his religion, but the pastor's argument was that my having a different faith would in itself push him in the wrong direction. He quoted excerpts from the Bible that supported his argument. With most Christians we spoke to, the same phrase came up over and over again, "Be ye not unequally yoked together with unbelievers." To me, those same verses, like most religious texts, could have been understood in a variety of ways. Cassius, a non-denominational Christian with Southern Baptist roots, struggled with his pastor's comments. I went to church with Cassius regularly, but the pastor refused to acknowledge or even look at me. After a few months, Cassius made the difficult decision to leave the church where the rest of his family worshiped and move to one I felt more comfortable attending.

As the months passed, I tried not to tell my parents about the pregnancy. I held out for as long as I could while Cassius and I tried to work things out between us. We decided to see a relationship counselor because we realized that whether or not we chose to be together, we would have to work out our differences if we were both going to play a role in raising our child. The counselor didn't have all of the answers and didn't tell us who was right or wrong. I guess that would have been too easy. Instead, we learned to communicate and really figure out what we were or weren't willing to compromise in order to make our relationship work. Our counselor supported our pursuit of an interfaith marriage, and through the experience we were able to share with each other the religious practices and beliefs we hoped to teach our child. For Cassius, it was important that we go to church every week for praise and worship. I wanted to teach our son Arabic and, when he is old enough, encourage him to fast with me throughout the month of *Ramadan*. As we started to come together as a team, we were willing to defend each other and stand up to the rest of the world in defense of our relationship.

It was no longer religion that stood between our union. It was pressure from our family, friends, and society as a whole. At that point, I decided I couldn't keep it from my parents any longer. I sat down with my sister who had known about the pregnancy from the very beginning, across from my dad and mom. As much as I try to block it out, I can't forget my dad's face. He didn't say anything. But in his eyes I could see myself as a lifetime's worth of disappointment. His face just collapsed. I can't remember what my mother said, or screamed, but I'm pretty sure it was a mouthful of expletives. She knew that Cassius and I had broken up, and *this* was the reason we were getting back together?! "There's no way that he's going to be in your life. How do you even know that you're really pregnant? Most women miscarry by three months. I'm sure you're going to have a miscarriage. Don't you dare tell anyone about this. We're not telling anyone!" followed by another torrent of cuss words. I can't even remember the rest of it. All I remember is my dad's face and my mom's explosion.

Shortly afterward, I began to receive emails from aunts and uncles who were astonished that I had gotten married. Almost as surprised as I was. My mother spread the news to her extended family and friends that I had married weeks before. Her plan was to announce a break-up shortly after I gave birth. In addition to trying to work out the drastic changes affecting my own life, I found myself defending a marriage that wasn't even real, one that I wasn't even ready to commit to. My relatives were telling me what a horrible mistake this was to marry a non-Muslim man and that I had to get out of it "before you get pregnant or something!" I ignored the emails, nodded through the face-to-face conversations, and did my best to disconnect from everyone who had an opinion on my scandalous, unbelievable, and non-existent nuptials. Now I could add liar to my list of offenses.

I cut myself off emotionally and physically for the next few months, while Cassius and I went to counseling and discussed marriage. I wasn't in contact with anyone who wasn't directly in front of me. Valentine's Day came and went and we were still talking about marriage without any conclusive plan. I decided to leave the studio apartment where I was living and move back in with my parents to save money. I didn't know where I would be when I gave birth, but I knew I couldn't do it alone if I wanted to take maternity leave.

Living at home was both difficult and helpful. I now had an hour-and-a-half commute to work, instead of a ten-minute one. I also had my mother cooking delicious home food for me and packing my lunches, even as she calculated and attempted to dictate every action or decision I made about my future. My mother comes from a culture and family that is very proud. She refused to marry my father unless he converted to Islam, and expected her children to do the same. She has always been stubborn and feisty, but her love is strong. The downfall is that sometimes she loves too hard, and in her attempt to protect us she ends up trying to control our lives. My dad was always the disciplinarian of the household when we were younger, but he knows when to step back and support our decisions as adults.

Growing up in rural New England, my family experienced varying levels of prejudice. My mom often enjoyed the extra attention brought about by her "exotic" background, and considered any negative interactions unavoidable because she accepted that racism was everywhere and you just had to deal with it. After September 11th, discrimination became much more blatant, and bigoted groups began to threaten us solely because of our faith. At that point, my mother started to buy into the idea that Islam and American culture were at odds with one another. She was convinced that her children were trying too hard to be American. It seemed to her that we were choosing America over Islam, and we couldn't possibly be both American and Muslim. All of a sudden, the liberal and open-minded approach to life and religion that she had raised us with changed form, and she began to regret her teachings. Once she perceived us as taking on an American identity and hence "losing" our Muslim identity, she approached us with a very conservative version of religion. Every conversation we had or choice we made became a debate about our loyalty to Islam. When it came to religion, and really any life choice we made, our mother became the authority in our household.

The first time Cassius saw my parents after I told them about the pregnancy, he asked my dad if he could speak with him privately. He wanted to formally apologize to my father about the situation. My mother caught wind of what was going on and was immediately offended by the gesture. She joined their meeting and, I can only imagine, started grilling Cassius. To this day, I still don't know what went on in that room; I just know that Cassius came out with a much better understanding of how my family works.

As spring break approached, the day before we left for a weekend in the snow, I went outside at 6 a.m. to go to work and found a giant green poster board outside of my parents' house. This poster board had directions on it telling me to follow clues throughout the day, and each clue would lead me closer to my "treasure." I spent the whole day following clues placed throughout the school where I worked, delivered by students and staff members, until the trail led me to Cassius' apartment. When I got there, he had cooked me a delicious meal and gave me a dozen multi-colored roses. After dinner, we got in the car and he drove me to my favorite beach and handed me my last clue. It was a build-a-bear monkey, and when I pressed his hand (as the clue told me to), the monkey said, in Cassius' voice, "Sumaya Cole, I love you, and I just wanted to know." Cassius kneeled down, revealed an emerald ring, and asked me to marry him.

I was happy—and scared. I didn't call anyone as we drove home. I didn't want to ruin the moment. But once we got back to his apartment, I decided to tell my mom because I would have to show her the ring when I got home anyway. I was nervous, but hoped she was prepared to handle it. I told her in one sentence. The phone clicked immediately. I never got a chance to hear her reaction. I know it's probably best I didn't.

Cassius and I left the next day to dance and play in the snow. We talked about a wedding, but didn't get into planning any details because we didn't want to ruin the excitement with logistics. When we got back, his family had a flurry of questions. His sister started looking up different places where we could have a very small ceremony near the beach.

The idea of having a wedding was daunting to me. We couldn't decide if we wanted to get married in two weeks, two months, or two years. We couldn't decide where to get married, who would come, or if we were even ready. I was now five months pregnant and starting to show. I didn't want to have a wedding in June when I was seven months pregnant, because I knew I couldn't invite anyone in my extended family or family friends. At that point, I was certain my mom wasn't planning on coming anyway. All of the anxiety piled up around me, and I couldn't figure out how to get around it.

I kept making excuses, and we never made any concrete plans. My mother threatened to disown me if we got married, saying it would shame her beyond repair. I pushed back with the fact that everyone already thought we were married anyway. What was the difference? She kept pressuring us to have a *nikah*, a Muslim ceremony, but not a legal one. In her eyes, that meant we would be married under Allah, but as long as we didn't sign any paperwork, we wouldn't have to commit to each other legally. A divorce would be easier that way, in her opinion, and she could still tell our family members that we had actually been married at one point. Cassius didn't see the difference between a Muslim ceremony and a legal ceremony—both were before Allah/God—and I couldn't imagine having a fake wedding before Allah. It didn't make sense to me, and didn't seem very Islamic. I wanted to fade away so someone else could deal with the mess I left.

It was mid-July and there was only a month and a half left before I was going to give birth. My son was due on September 14th, and I realized I would not be able to return to work the following school year. This was probably the scariest factor of all—I was going to have a baby and no job. I was going to have to rely on someone to make things work. If I waited to get married until our son was born, Cassius and I would have to live apart for the first few months of our child's life. Finally, Cassius and I made a decision—a concrete, steadfast, no-turning-back decision. We found an apartment that we both loved and signed a lease. On a Sunday, I called my brother's girlfriend and told her, "We want to get married on Friday. Do you think you can help us pull it together?"

We found a man who conducted weddings on the Palos Verdes peninsula on the cliffs overlooking the ocean. There were no seats, but we weren't expecting many guests to show up with a week's notice, so we didn't mind. We called our families and let them know our plans. I decided to tell just my father and let him convey the message to my mom: I was scared to hear her response. I should have known my mother better than to think she wouldn't come to my wedding. She even bought a new outfit for the occasion.

Two days before the wedding, Cassius' sister and brother-in-law stopped by—she sat on the couch with me while her husband stood by the door. "We've spoken a lot about it and we really want to come, but we can't. We can't come to your wedding ceremony because it's against our religious beliefs." They had spoken to their pastor, the same one who wouldn't give Cassius his blessing, who told them that as believing Christians, they could not support our marriage. The pastor told them that they had to take a stand against it to save their own souls, and so they did. As they were telling us this, tears started running down my face. I could see that Cassius was hurt, but all he said was that he understood their decision. He had paid for his sister's honeymoon, and she wasn't going to support him on one of the biggest days of his life.

That night, in our new apartment, I started to feel contractions like I hadn't felt before. They were strong, and they were coming every few minutes. I tried to wake Cassius up. I tried everything short of hitting him with pots and pans, but Cassius wouldn't budge. So I ended up writing him a note and driving myself to the hospital at 1:00 a.m. When I got there, they hooked me up to a fetal monitor and gave me a shot to stop my contractions. I had gone into pre-term labor. After four hours, I got another shot, and a flurry of questions from nurses wondering why I had come there by myself. They discharged me, encouraging me to have someone else drive me next time, "just in case!" When I got back in my car to drive home, Cassius called me in hysterics, wondering where I could be and why in the world I hadn't woken him up. I was too tired to debate. I promised to break out the pots and pans next time around.

Our wedding was the next day. I encouraged Cassius to invite a few of his closest friends to support him in place of his sister and her husband. My contractions had slowed down, but didn't stop. I was tired, exhausted, and had very little energy to put into preparing myself for the "big day." All I cared about was that I found a dress that I could squeeze into. I bought a pair of gold flip flops that day, and I went to a bootleg nail salon to get an $18 manicure-pedicure with yellow nail polish. I was convinced that it was gold when I picked up the bottle. My sister did my hair and make-up while her son ran around. My contractions continued, stronger and closer together the later it got. I considered going back to the hospital, but I knew that if we didn't make this happen right now, it might not ever happen. So I pushed through.

My sister and I showed up forty-five minutes late for the ceremony, and luckily they decided not to start without us. A dreary coastal sky cleared up right before sunset. We had a quiet, beautiful ceremony with (almost) all of the people we loved. Cassius and I laughed together at how crazy this was and cried a little in relief. When our ceremony was over, my contractions were coming every five minutes, but I fought through them and smiled for all of the pictures.

I overheard my mom talking about how the non-denominational vows used the word "Lord," complaining that it was a Christian ceremony. I acted like I didn't hear it. We were very particular about what we used for vows and there was nothing religion-specific about it. Still, I had a feeling she might find something wrong with it. She had wanted me to find an *imam* to perform the ceremony. But after reaching out to every resource I could find, there was no *imam* or Muslim man who was willing to perform a ceremony between a Christian man and Muslim woman. We couldn't ask any Muslim men we knew because, well, on top of my scandalous marriage, I was eight-and-a-half-months pregnant, and everyone in our community already thought I had gotten married back in February.

When we left the site of the ceremony, our small pool of guests joined us at a nice Italian restaurant for dinner. My brother's girlfriend had made it a quaint, yet beautiful event. My parents covered the cost of the wedding and with my sister's help, we booked a suite at a beautiful resort on the Palos Verdes cliffs. We smiled and laughed through the delicious dinner, even though my insides were tightening and twisting with every contraction. Before our wedding cake came out, we decided we were going to have to make a trip back to the hospital. After thanking everyone for coming, setting my parents up to stay in our suite for the night, and quickly cutting the cake—which I still can't find pictures of—we left the party to rush to the hospital. There were more shots, metal devices, fetal monitors, and ultrasounds. We left early the next morning, wearing our wedding clothes, and with nurses throwing rose petals into the elevator.

In early September, during one of my many visits to the hospital, the condition of my pregnancy worsened. My contractions led to drops in my son's heartbeat. He wasn't reacting well and hadn't been growing in the past few weeks. He was under-developed and under-nourished and I wasn't dilating when they induced me. A day later, the labor was still not progressing. My doctor told me that as much as I wanted to have an all-natural birth, I would have to have a C-section if I didn't want to pose any further risk to my son's health. That's all he needed to say. We were in the operating room half an hour later.

My son was a miracle—alien-like, overwhelming, and beautiful all at once. We spent five days in the hospital because of all of the complications that followed his birth. He was underweight and had low blood sugar and jaundice, to name a few of the ailments he endured. I remember the night he had to lie under a blue light with goggles for hours, screaming. All Cassius and I could do was pray. His prayers were in English and mine in Arabic, but we prayed together.

We finally left the hospital. We were a little family. I stayed home with our son while Cassius went to work. He was sick all the time. I would cry late at night by myself trying to breastfeed him, not knowing what I could possibly do to help him anymore. We didn't find out until later that he was severely allergic to what I was eating—milk and nuts—he was anemic, and had asthma. Our son's first year was the hardest year of my life. I was without a job, newly married, and trying to survive motherhood with a baby who was chronically ill. Cassius and I seriously struggled. I wondered if I had made the right choice in marrying him, or if I had just gone through with it out of desperation. I was depressed and didn't know how to dig myself out of it. All the while, Cassius was a cushion. We fought on and off, but Cassius spent most of the time listening, understanding, supporting, and compromising. He was the sole reason we survived that year.

As our anniversary approached and my mom started accepting the fact that Cassius and I were really married, she started pushing us to celebrate with a real wedding reception. She had never gotten a chance to host what she called *her* wedding. It was becoming clear to her that Cassius and I were both in it for the long haul, and her fear of me "selling out" to American culture and rejecting my own faith had subsided. I resisted at first. Who was going to come? Our original wedding had brought with it so much drama and turmoil; I didn't want to have to go through that all over again. But after talking to Cassius, we decided to do it for ourselves, to celebrate in a way that we never had the chance to before. We invited family and friends from South Africa, Saudi Arabia, Tanzania, England, Oman, New York, Texas, and more. My mom tried to convince us to have a ceremony again, but that was drama I wasn't willing to rekindle. My mom, sister, cousins, and friends helped plan a beautiful *henna night* and an amazing event for our reception at an Armenian restaurant in LA. It was the most multi-cultural wedding many of our guests had ever attended. We had 175 friends and family members from all around the world, including *all* of our loved ones.

Cassius' sister and her husband offered to pay for all of the flowers in an effort, I think, to make up for their lack of support the year before. It had been hard to rebuild our relationship in the past year, and this gesture was the beginning of our reconciliation.

The wedding reception was amazing, and it felt like Cassius and I finally got to take a minute out of the crazy turn our lives had taken to actually celebrate our union.

At one point between celebrations, I overheard my cousins saying that I was a lost cause already, and that they had to concentrate on our son to make sure that he was raised Muslim. By this time, I was used to people's opinions, and I was confident in my choice to commit to my husband with all that entailed. Cassius and I were doing everything in our power to support each other in our own practices and teachings. We decided to demonstrate our beliefs, walk the walk, and let our son make his own religious choices based on what he learns from his parents. Who knows how it will work out, but just as many children who are purposefully raised Christian end up being Atheist, or are actively raised Muslim and become Buddhist. Children will make their own choices in the end, and we intend to provide him with all of the tools that he'll need to make that choice. Until then, we're learning, little by little, to accept each other's beliefs and to continue loving each other through our disagreements.

The other day, after my eyes were hurting, Cassius said "Your eyes look good today, *mashallah*." He had joined me at a meeting held by a progressive Muslim group in L.A. and was starting to see that the images and politics he had witnessed in mainstream media were not representative of my Islam. Before we were married, I was worried that the person I loved would think the most important thing to me was fundamentally wrong, or even evil. It was scary exposing him to my religion, not knowing how he might react. Now I practice my faith in confidence, beside my husband, and we don't allow surface-level differences to distract us from our shared values.

I pray *shahada*, our declaration of faith, with my son whenever we get into the car, and before dinner, I start with *bismillah* and Cassius continues our prayers in English. Before we sleep, Cassius kneels by the bed and I bow toward Mecca, each of us humbled by an almighty power. His prayers are motivated by the story of Christ, who sacrificed his life to save the human race. The power of Allah, as I see it, is described in the *surah* that begins, "*Qul huwa Allahu ahad*," (Say he is Allah, the one and only). Our prayers may appear to contradict each other, but they share a purpose, to praise God and direct us along His path. And so, we climb into bed each night, together, with a renewed spirit and mind.

Finding My Religion

By Patricia Dunn

Fifteen years ago, I converted from Catholicism to Islam. My mother still doesn't understand my choice, but there's not a day that I regret it.

I'm not the same woman I was at twenty-seven when I told my mother, "Ma, I can't eat the pasta fagioli." (She'd made it with bacon.) I'm not the same woman who lied when she said, "I didn't become Muslim because of Ahmed."

My mother believes that for women, most problems and solutions begin and end with the man in her life. But back then there was no way this feminist would admit to anyone—including herself and especially not her mother—that she had converted because of a man.

Today, at forty-two, and secure in my faith, I can admit that if it weren't for Ahmed—now my ex-husband—the word "Islam" would probably still conjure up images of black-cloaked women and melodramatic Sally Field movies in my head. After all, I am my mother's daughter.

The day I left my Italian-Bronx neighborhood to go to college, I knew my communion and confession days were over. I was never going to let Jesus stick to the roof of my mouth again. There were too many contradictions for me in Catholicism. Why was my never-miss-Sunday-mass father excommunicated after he and my mother divorced—especially when *she* was the one having the affair? How could the pope have an Olympic-size swimming pool while millions of his people were starving? And how could I tolerate the Church's position on abortion and women's rights?

By the time I transferred from Barnard to UCLA, I was a lapsed Catholic who wanted nothing to do with organized religion. But I needed to believe in something.

During my years at UCLA, I spent more hours making fliers, organizing demonstrations and making phone calls—and once or twice bail—than I spent studying. I defended clinics under attack by anti-abortionists; I worked for funding for the homeless and against nuclear testing; I traveled to Nicaragua to build houses and to Arizona to herd sheep for Navajos fighting to keep their land.

I tried to change the world one cause at a time.

In the summer of 1988, I interned at *The Nation* magazine's Washington office. While researching a story about Mubarak Awad, a Palestinian-American psychologist and founder of the Palestinian Center for Non-Violence, the president of the American-Arab Anti-Discrimination Committee invited me to go on a student delegation to the Occupied Territories. Two weeks after returning to UCLA from the West Bank and Gaza I gave a talk to fifty students about my experience. I explained how the *intifada* had propelled women into major leadership roles. How women-run factories and businesses were building an infrastructure for a future state.

At the back of the room stood a man, six feet tall with bright red hair. He held his hand to his chin, and his focus on me helped me focus. When I finished, he applauded louder than anyone else. I was relieved the talk had been a success—at least no one from the audience had shouted out, "Arab-loving whore!".

The man waited until I had gathered my notes and walked off the stage before approaching me.

"Brilliant speech," he said.

I thanked him, trying not to blush.

"My name is Ahmed," he said, extending his hand. But I already knew who he was.

He was president of the Muslim Students Association and, like me, he wrote a column for the school paper, where we were both slotted "on the left." I was a fan.

This was a guy who knocked on every door in Isla Vista, in Santa Barbara, Calif., to campaign for Jesse Jackson. But that day, when he smiled a win-me-over smile, I thought the same thing I'd wondered whenever I read his column, "How could a smart, socially-conscientious guy be a Muslim—be a part of any organized religion?" He was a feminist. A feminist Muslim—wasn't that an oxymoron?

As Ahmed and I spent the next several years deepening our friendship—and eventually marrying—I returned again and again to those questions. He mostly stood out of my way. It didn't matter to him if I was Catholic or Muslim or Jewish or Marxist (though he thought Marx grossly underestimated the seduction of capitalism). Ahmed wanted me to come to my own conclusions about Islam. After all, it was what he'd had to do. He'd been born into a Muslim family, but after they emigrated from Cairo to Los Angeles, Islam played little visible role in their lives. It wasn't until Ahmed read the Qur'an for the first time in college that he helped his parents reconnect with their faith.

I studied Islam in order to debate Ahmed and his belief system, but the more I learned, the more I found how greatly I had underestimated my own ignorance. Mine wasn't a hit-you-over-the-head epiphany, but rather a slow and steady stream of aha's.

The feminist in me aha'd when she realized that in the Qur'an God is neither male nor female. The scholar in me aha'd at the various interpretations and schools of thought within Islam—most of which depict the religion as a social and constantly changing belief system, rather than the fixed, dogmatic one the government of Saudi Arabia would have the world believe.

The Christian in me aha'd when she read in the Qur'an how those who do good deeds are in God's grace. And the scared Bronx girl in me aha'd at the Qur'an's refrain that God is "merciful and compassionate"—until, eventually, the scared Bronx girl was no more.

But it was the social activist in me who aha'd the loudest when she got a deeper understanding of *jihad* (a term that has been grossly misinterpreted in the media). *Jihad* is a word with many meanings, but foremost it describes one's personal and inner struggle to live a just life, a life in which one is obligated to defend those who cannot defend themselves. Wasn't that what I had always tried to commit my life to—fighting, or, more accurately, struggling, for justice?

Who knows? Maybe I would have remained a Catholic if I had discovered the Catholic Worker movement or Catholics for a Free Choice earlier in life—organizations whose missions emphasize economic and social justice. Maybe I would have remained a Catholic if the one priest who talked and listened to me when I was thirteen had done so face to face and not in some dark box (and if he had, along with hearing me confess and granting me absolution, counseled me about surviving adolescence). Then there was the question of Jesus. It had always been hard for me to believe God took human form. But it was as a Muslim that I learned what an incredible prophet he was—the epitome of the social activist.

After years of questioning Ahmed about everything, I found my answers in Islam. But as a convert I had to work for everything I believed. I was constantly translating, not only the language of the Qur'an, but the rituals too. It was hard to trust that one could have a one-to-one relationship with God, and I still believed I needed an intermediary, some authority, someone more worthy to intervene on my behalf. So I turned to the "real" Muslim, the one born into faith, for all my answers. I made Ahmed my teacher, my priest.

While equality was the rule in every other aspect of our lives, when it came to matters of faith, I wanted Ahmed to call the shots. When we prayed, though he encouraged—often insisted—that I lead the prayer; I refused. To me, Ahmed was the authority. Besides, he sounded so beautiful when he recited the Qur'an in Arabic. I wanted him to give me all the answers, and when he refused, my questions turned into childish badgering: "Are you sure if you swallow accidentally while you brush your teeth, that doesn't break your fast during *Ramadan*?"

It wasn't until my son was born that I truly grew up into Islam. Ali was seven weeks premature, and small enough to fit in the palms of his father's hands. The doctors told us Ali couldn't go home until he was able to regulate his own body temperature. I could hardly swallow as I watched my son in his plastic incubator, trailing tubes and wires to help him breathe. It had taken years of trying and fertility testing for Ahmed and me to get pregnant: I couldn't believe God would take our son from us now. I felt like a kid again—swept back in time to age twelve, when I'd been convinced God had killed my friend Barbara by giving her leukemia for no reason at all.

Desperate for hope, I saw breast-feeding as the one way I could help Ali heal—but he was too weak to latch on. So on the first day of his life, instead of a newborn suckling at my breast, I nursed an electric pump (on loan from the hospital) to increase my milk supply. Then—somehow—the loud methodical chugging of the pump's motor helped to drown out my fear. "In the name of God, the Benevolent, the Merciful..." I began reciting the first *sura* in the

Qur'an. "...It is You we serve, to You we turn for help..." There, alone in the hospital, I spoke to God for the first time, one to one, with no intermediary. And I understood that the God I was talking to was compassionate and merciful.

Two weeks later, Ali began to nurse. The day I took him home in his oversize blue-striped onesie, I knew God had heard me.

Though I still love my son's father, Ahmed and I have been legally separated for a year now. There were, in the end, some questions that Islam could not answer. Thanks to our faith, a lot of prayer—and yes, some therapy—we have remained friends and continue to raise our son together.

I'm not the same Muslim I was fifteen years ago, but I am still a Muslim. Last week, after all these years, when I told my mother that Ali couldn't eat her baked beans because they were made with pork, her response was the same as ever.

"That's ridiculous," she said. Then she mumbled, "Well, let's see what you believe when the next guy comes around."

I didn't respond. My belief in Islam may have started with a man, but it continues with me, and it's never-ending.

Reprinted from *Salon.com*

Living Up To My Name

By Daayiee Abdullah

I was born the same year that *Brown v. Board of Education* became the law of the land, and my life has incorporated many changes that have reconfigured and reshaped the American landscape we live in today. Whether it is race relations, women's rights, gay rights, or building a multi-ethnic and multicultural America, I have been there. Now, at the turn of the 21st century, I am involved in the reshaping of ancient perspectives within the Islamic faith as an openly gay Muslim *imam*.

My journey into Islam began when I got a fellowship to learn Chinese from Georgetown University. I started the program, and within nine months, I was at Beijing University. In China, some of my classmates were Uyghurs, a Turkic ethnic group living in the northwestern part of the country. Uyghurs are predominantly Muslim. On one occasion, some of my Uyghur friends asked me if I knew anything about Islam. One of my brothers was a member of the Nation of Islam, and I told them about that. They were quick to tell me about their kind of Islam.

The Chinese Muslims had been Muslims since the lifetime of Prophet Muhammad. Over a period spanning five dynasties, Islam evolved to become a part of Chinese history, and because of their unique culture, the Chinese Muslims were not influenced by the larger Muslim histories of the Middle East and South Asia.

When one of my Chinese friends invited me to the local mosque, I accepted. There are nearly fifty thousand mosques in China. The Huaisheng mosque in Guangzhou had been built just twenty years after the Prophet's death. It wasn't the first mosque in China, but it's the oldest one still in use. This means some Chinese had been Muslim longer than some Arabs!

One Friday after class, we headed to the Cow Street mosque in Beijing. My classmates showed me how to do the ritual washing before entering. Then, I looked at the Qur'ans, which were in both Arabic and Chinese. Shortly afterwards, the leader gave the lecture in Arabic and Mandarin. This was before I learned Arabic. When I heard it in Chinese, it made perfect sense to me. He explained that Islam was a religion of peace and instructed us to focus our work on becoming a better person, not on rules and regulations. It was a profoundly moving message but rendered in a simple and uncomplicated way.

And so began my fascination with Islam.

I continued to go to the mosque from time to time. There was something about Islam I was attracted to. God in Islam sounded calm and merciful. A lot of the questions I had inside of me began to slowly find answers. And the gentleness of the Chinese Muslims further reinforced my growing attraction to the faith. I didn't convert immediately, but being more closely drawn to the ideals of Islam, I knew I was onto something important in my life.

There was something about praying the Muslim way that made me want to learn more about Islam. I enjoyed especially how I felt afterwards. As a Christian, whenever I would pray, I felt that I was supplicating all the time. But in Islam, whenever I would do the *sujud*, the part where you touch your forehead onto the floor, I experienced a full sense of surrender. And as I read and talked to people, I learned that whenever I had a question for God, I should release it, surrender it over to God. Then, one of two things would happen. Either God would, by the end of the prayer, provide me with an inspirational reply, or I'd be left with such inner peace I could wait for the answer.

Of course, I knew the prevailing view of the community was that homosexuality is wrong within the Islamic belief system. But that just didn't seem to be correct to me. My Chinese friends told me that the Chinese have a long history of acceptance towards homosexuality. For example, the "cut sleeve" story is a famous love story between Emperor Xiao Ai and his male lover Dong Xiang. They were sleeping together one afternoon. When Emperor Ai woke up and decided to get up, he realized that part of his pajama sleeve was under the sleeping Dong Xiang. Rather than disturb Dong Xiang, he cut his sleeve off.

Since the Chinese had been Muslim for many centuries, it seemed to me that they had real information. The Islam of ancient times was different from the Islam that we were getting in the modern age. I said to myself that I had to find the information that says homosexuality is acceptable. So, I continued to go to the mosque throughout the year and learned a lot more about Islam in China. I even started wearing the little caps as a sign that I was Muslim, particularly to the Uyghurs, who were famous for selling lamb skewers on the streets as vendors.

After that year, I went to Taiwan for further language study, where I ran into the Saudi or *Wahhabi* version of Islam, but I also had a number of Arab, African and Southeast Asian classmates with whom I could talk about Islam. The Saudis had a nice big mosque in Taipei, but their Islamic practices were far more strict than what I had learned in China. It was not always easy to sit through the sermons at that mosque. In Taiwan, it was how *Wahhabis* practiced Islam. Theirs was a very restrictive interpretation of the same book. It really put me off. In China, I never heard hate-filled sermons, but in Taiwan, at the Saudi mosque, it was a frequent theme. In China, I felt like I was accepted as an equal, while in Taiwan, I was often treated like an outsider, too inexperienced in Islam, and as a convert, someone who should not use his own intellect to question Islamic *fiqh*.

Additionally, the son of the *imam* in Taiwan had recently returned from Saudi Arabia because he had been caught on several occasions having sexual relations with his male classmates—something that brought shame to his family. He was often sequestered and, when in public, his behavior was strictly scrutinized, so I never got an opportunity to speak to him alone. I wanted to share with him that I was also gay and express my feelings and experiences while living in China. He experienced visceral, gut-wrenching hatred as a gay Muslim, and I knew it would not be an easy task to open discussions on being gay and Muslim in *Wahhabi* circles.

When I came back to the United States, I did two things.

First, I officially converted to Islam, signing the conversion papers with my chosen conversion name. While in China, my friends had given me a Chinese name—Tang Da Yi, (唐大义). The Tang Dynasty in Chinese history, 635 CE to around 935 CE, was the most peaceful literary period in China; thus they gave me the last name "Tang" (唐). "Da" (大) means big and "Yi" (义) means virtue. So my name became "the peaceful man of great virtue." When I converted, I wanted an Arabic name similar to Da Yi. In Arabic, Daayiee (داعي) means the person who calls back to the faith, or the one who proselytizes, which fits me perfectly.

Second, I started Arabic studies. Luckily for me, I had gotten a head start learning the Arabic alphabet and numbers in Taiwan from Arab friends from Libya, Morocco, Syria, Jordan, the Gulf, and Saudi Arabia. With Chinese and English as our common languages, they taught me the Arabic basics that would help me later in the Middle East. After the first school year of Arabic, I went to the American University in Cairo for a year, then to Jordan for another year, and finally, to Syria for a year. After returning to Georgetown for my final year of school, I applied for and received a full tuition scholarship to D.C. School of Law.

There, I was active in the gay student association. The Muslims had difficulties with me because of my sexual orientation and the gay students had an issue with my faith. Toward the end of my first year of law school, University of Michigan reoffered me a fellowship to continue my graduate studies and allowed me to substitute my electives with law school courses.

The two years went by quickly at the University of Michigan because I was reunited with several of my Arab friends from Cairo and Amman. During my time at Michigan, Siraj Kugle, author of "Homosexuality in Islam," and I met at a Middle East conference at Duke University. Several years later, we would reconnect via Al-Fatiha Foundation, the organization for LGBTQ Muslims.

I graduated and practiced law. Though I enjoyed the profession for a while, it eventually wore me down. I was becoming aware that I had a different path, but what it was had yet to be revealed to me. So when I had an opportunity to go to Saudi Arabia for a few years to teach for the Saudi Royal Air Force, I took it. Being Muslim and a speaker of Arabic, I was a very good match for the three-year position.

In Saudi Arabia, I would see *Wahhabism* in its fullest form, learn about it first hand, and judge how it compared to my earlier learning about Islam. Working there would give me access to books that were not available to me in the United States, as well as courses at the universities. Therefore, in Saudi Arabia, I was able to do the research to represent an alternative voice for queer Muslims. I did my first paper on a homosexual-positive interpretation of the Qur'an. After working and making friends off the American compound, I took weekly classes at the local Islamic center where I met a scholar in Islam who had graduated first in his class at the Prophet's School in Medina—a real honor.

Through our long-term association and friendship, I had the opportunity to read and discuss texts that helped me come to the conclusion that interpreters were the culprits in maligning queer Muslims.

My first effort was to look at various authors of different Qur'ans in different languages, including English-Arabic, Chinese-Arabic, and Arabic-Arabic Qur'ans with *tafseer* (explanations). I wanted to be able to compare not only interpretations, but also the biases of the interpreters. When I realized how the translators interpreted the Qur'an, I knew I was onto something.

Of course, how the Qur'an gets translated is the cause of much dispute between the orthodox and the progressive Muslims in our community—some of these translators do not meet the "sniff" test. Under some readings, women, children, sexual minorities, foreign workers, and non-Sunni Muslim believers suffer from misguided interpretations—definitely a problem for Muslims generally and, more specifically, for these groups of believers who were not empowered to protect their rights.

Islamic history covers nearly 1450 years. Relying upon the tomes of ancient thinkers, ideals appropriate for those ancient times are too often viewed as precious jewels of an ancient and pristine Islam. No matter how much pressure these gems of Islamic thought have faced over time, we should not adhere to them as presented, as if they were appropriate for modern times. We cannot, as thinking individuals, mindlessly and blindly inculcate and apply ancient teachings on the assumption that everything that is ancient is good.

Next, I researched Islamic marriage and gender bias. I examined how the standards for marriage could be applied to all Muslims who are consenting adults, not just a male- female couple. During the last year of my contract in Saudi Arabia, I was put in touch with Faisal Alam, the founder of Al-Fatiha Foundation in Washington, D.C. I sent Faisal a copy of my research and his response was enthusiastic. He said he felt my study was one of the keys to the discussions on homosexuality within Islam.

I returned to the United States a couple of weeks before New Year 2000, amidst all the fear and madness associated with Y2K. I was also about to make another transition in my life, becoming a gay activist for queer Muslims in the West. I began working with Faisal and others under the Al-Fatiha banner in different parts of the United States, Canada, and Europe, where I attended many conferences and meetings. Eventually, international sister chapters were established in many parts of the world.

I eventually became an Al-Fatiha board member, and took on the role of religious advisor. I knew I needed to become a *sheikh* in Islamic law in order to make an impact. I wanted to help queer Muslims become comfortable with alternative readings and interpretations of the Qur'an that promoted a positive response to queers. In September 2000, I entered the Graduate School of Islamic Social Sciences (GSISS) in northern Virginia, the same school that trains *imams* and chaplains for the U.S. military and hospitals throughout the United States. I studied there for two and a half years and earned a master's degree in Shariah Sciences and Qur'anic Interpretation.

My mentor at GSISS, Dr. Taha, taught me a lot. He would tell me, "Daayiee, don't think of yourself as an *imam*; you're a *sheikh* (scholar). You're an educated person (in languages and law), so you should be part of academia." That was what I aspired to—to become a scholar in Islam.

But when some of the people at GSISS found out I was gay, I became *persona non grata* at the school. It was March 2003, and I only had a couple of papers to turn in, as I had completed the course work. I asked for an extension, but when I did turn my papers in, they kicked me out of the school, claiming that I "was not the quality of student that should be involved in the Muslim community." Because they were located in Virginia where many anti-gay religious institutions are based, such as Jerry Falwell's Liberty University, GSISS had full reign to discriminate on the basis of sexual orientation. As my attorney said, because they didn't receive federal money, under federal law, I couldn't sue them for discrimination. When the GSISS was eventually closed down two years after 9/11, a number of the professors and staff left, returning to the Middle East to teach.

I took this episode in my life as a stepping stone to reach another level to strengthen queer Muslims. Even without a degree, I had my union card,—the knowledge to utilize these sciences in Qur'anic interpretation and research. I just needed to do more to develop the *shari'ah* (way of life) and *fiqh* (jurisprudence methods) process as it related to gay Muslims.

I did my work through the Al-Fatiha movement, and eventually the need for specific services for queer Muslims grew, e.g., *janazah* prayers, pastoral counseling, same-sex *nikahs*. That is when the concept of my being an *imam* became a necessity. I moderate a group called Muslim Gay Men, something I have been doing continuously for nearly eleven years now. Muslim Gay Men was the perfect forum where I could test my theories and eventually get involved in heavy-weight theological discussion with lay persons and others who professed they had studied in similar institutions of higher learning in other parts of the world. In that very early time period, there was heated debate on the issues of homosexuality in an Islamic context. So groups like StraightWay Foundation in the United Kingdom and other groups of anti- or ex-gays would come en masse and join our discussions. Then they would attempt to overrun the group with their negativity and false information and belief systems. I was ready for them. I showed them the errors of their scholarship. I showed them that the information they passed on was inaccurate, misleading, or just plain false. These homophobes wanted to depend on ancient scholars, which was fine with me, as I had the tools to do that kind of research. I told them, "If you really want to discuss the subject, then let's go back to the ancients and do it the way they did." We could discover what Islam would allow and what it would not—but it was not as easy as they thought, and they were ill prepared for the onslaught of information I provided. I often silenced them in their tracks.

In the end, they would always leave with their tails between their legs because they didn't know what they were talking about or based their arguments on regurgitated scholarship without knowing the historical background and Qur'anic information Islamic jurists used. Many of them didn't know Arabic, its grammar, and other things of this nature. Through these debates, I made a good name for the group. My notoriety started and developed in the queer and progressive Muslim communities.

Soon I was giving lectures, going to various events, and speaking about homosexuality within an Islamic context. My efforts were not limited to gay issues only. I also spoke out about women's rights, sexual minorities and children—basically, holding up the United Nations Declaration of Human Rights as a standard to which Islam had to rise in order for it to be relevant for modern times. Eventually, I was not only going to Al-Fatiha conferences around the country and internationally, I also began lecturing at colleges and universities. I started working with gay organizations like the Human Rights Campaign and the National Gay and Lesbian Task Force.

At the same time, I was also involved in the progressive Muslim movement. Progressives have helped many come out of the darkness of family and community shame because they expand on Islamic themes. Progressives know it is not Allah that prevents peaceful coexistence between humankind; it is humankind that judges and promotes separation. Progressive Muslim thought gives largesse to build communities that can include Muslims who are not traditionally accepted and build peace, intra-religiously and inter-religiously between Muslims and non-Muslims. Progressives demonstrate to orthodox believers that alternative paths to living out our faith are not limited to only the interpretations of the orthodox, no matter how ancient or "authoritative" the orthodox make them appear.

I was straddling two different Islamic-based movements, queer Muslims and progressive Muslims. I was not always welcomed in the progressive movement because I was gay, and from the point of view of some, considered to be outside the framework of Islam because I was willingly committing a "sin" in their eyes.

I received emails from distraught teenagers and young adults, and I was able to respond to most of their questions rather easily. A few years later, at the National Youth Advocacy conference, a young lady approached me and said, "You're Imam Daayiee, aren't you?" She went on, "Well, you may not remember me, but I wrote you a couple of years ago... And you kept me from committing suicide." I didn't remember her specifically. There were so many young people I had corresponded with at that time. When I heard those words, and so many comments like that, I knew I was doing the right thing.

I could see that I was helping people better understand themselves and refrain from doing something drastic within their lives. No matter what anyone else said, this was the right thing to do. It was during this process of development and growth that I began to settle into the role of *imam*. I said to myself, "Let me do this and see where it will take me." Until today, I have served around ten years as an *imam* within Al-Fatiha, and to the global queer Muslim movement. I share that distinction with Muhsin Hendricks, whom I do quite a bit of work with in different parts of the world. For the past year, I have served as a leader of a mosque in Washington, D.C.

I didn't seek out the role of *imam*. In fact, I was a bit put off by it because my goal was to become a *sheikh* within the faith. But the gay Muslim community needed someone in the community that could help them deal with issues of their religious faith and religious beliefs, and so I became an *imam* out of necessity.

The community I serve in Washington, D.C. is not predominantly one group. It is made up of straight, male and female, transgender, gay—the whole spectrum of people come for worship services. We also have interfaith meetings with progressive Jews and Christians—and we enjoy having events where we share our commonalities—the Abrahamic faith—and also our connectedness as Americans. We follow a concept developed by El-Tawhid Juma Prayer Center, which is located in Toronto, where, at their *iftaar* in 2004, I led a group of men and women praying side by side like they do in Mecca. In our mosques and centers, women call *adhan* and women lead prayer. This was the atmosphere I had learned under Dr. Taha at the GSISS, where they were training women to become *imams*. It wasn't strange for me to worship this way, and I encouraged others to do the same. One of the goals of our D.C. mosque is to create a model that can be replicated in other parts of the world. Our sacred space is similar to El-Tawhid's format, so the *masjid* is named Masjid an-Nur Al-Isslaah, which means the Light of Reformation Mosque, a member of the El-Tawhid Jum'ah Circle. And it is the first one to be led by an openly gay *imam*.

I am thankful for having had all of those wonderful experiences to bring me to this point in my life. What continues to give me the energy and verve to continue is the hope and desire of the numerous young people, rejecting aggressive orthodox Islamic ideals, to live their lives by the standards of human rights, freedom of speech even in debating Islamic tenets, and peaceful coexistence.

Now, I encourage all LGBTQ people, and everyone else, to look for their *iqraa* moment. *Iqraa* refers to the passage in the Qur'an first revealed to Prophet Muhammad that says, "You who were created from a clot of blood, recite." It means to recite from your own understanding who is your creator. I had my *iqraa* moment while seated at the Cow Street mosque in Beijing, China in the early 1980s, where I was transformed from a non-Muslim into a member of the Islamic community of believers, who happened to be my Uyghur classmates. My spheres of understanding and influence reach farther than I could have imagined ten years ago. The limited shades of gray cannot cloud the rainbow of Allah's variegated meanings. I find inclusivity among Allah's creation, covering the depth and breath of Allah's message deeply within my being.

Once you have your connection, once you recite and know that this is God who is talking to you, you're connected. Who can tell you that you're not right? It's through that process that I encourage all people, no matter your faith, to seek that moment with God. Be patient, and when God knocks, answer.

The Photovoice Project: An Interview with Rab Razzak

By Ani Zonneveld

The Photovoice Project recently had an exhibit of photos taken by young black men from some of the toughest neighborhoods in Los Angeles (LA). Their personal stories and reflection moved me and half the hall of about 100 people to tears. There was so much pain followed by so much strength from their stories. The Photovoice Project is a unique story of service to our community and a story of a man who went out of his way to help others unlike him in the true spirit of "love thy neighbor."

Ani Zonneveld: Tell us a bit about your background.

Rab Razzak: I was born in Bangladesh and was raised by my maternal grandparents in Bangladesh until I was five years old. My parents left my sister and me under their care when I was two as they moved to America in search of the American dream. My parents moved to Paterson, New Jersey—a rough, urban setting in northern New Jersey that was a haven for immigrants because of job opportunities. Somehow, my parents made ends meet. They were able to provide us with shelter, food for a family of six, and a decent education; all on a factory worker's salary.

I attended public elementary school. Besides Christianity, Sunni Islam is all the religion I knew. I attended a Catholic high school where I learned a lot more about Islam because we were instructed in the three Abrahamic faiths. This is where I learned to appreciate the similarities between our religions.

What is your professional field?

I was trained in internal medicine and currently practice hospital medicine and palliative care at Cedars-Sinai Medical Center. Hospital medicine is a professional field where a physician practices medicine only in the hospital setting. Palliative care is a relatively new subspecialty of medicine that deals with providing support to patients who are recently diagnosed with a life-threatening disease and helping them deal with end of life issues, spirituality, pain management, and hospice.

Recently you teamed up with your wife, Nazleen Bharmal, on a project—The Young Black Men's Photovoice Project. Tell us about it.

The Young Black Men's Photovoice Project (www.blackmensphotovoice.org) is a community-based, participatory research project. We provided cameras to young black males in Los Angeles County to take photographs of and discuss factors associated with their transition to manhood. Twelve participants, between the ages of sixteen and twenty-six, completed a three-month period of taking and pile-sorting photos, and developing their themes and sub-themes. They identified four major themes influential in their transition—struggles, social supports and inspiration, the role of sports, and the LA lifestyle.

We targeted these young men because this age is a vulnerable period in young men's lives, particularly young black men in urban settings. They previously had not been able to express feelings and events in their life course in a constructive way. They realized there was a deficit in their growing up with very few (if any) positive male role models. This men's group provided male models, including two other professional black males who helped moderate the men's group.

How does this project relate to health issues?

The Photovoice process is based on health promotion principles that aim to educate and empower community through photography. Simply put, if you feel empowered, you do more to take care of yourself and to get your life and health together.

Just consider some startling statistics related to the health issues of black men:

- Homicide is the number-one killer of black males between the ages of fifteen and twenty-four. 80% of homicides are at the hands of another black person.[6]

- Black men represent just over 6% of the population, but comprise 35% of drug arrests, 55% of drug convictions, and 74% of drug prisoners.[7]

- 40% of men of color are functionally illiterate.[8]

- By one estimate, 70% of those incarcerated in state and federal prisons are functionally illiterate or read below the eighth-grade level.[9]

- 32% of black males born in 2001 can expect to spend time in prison over the course of their lifetime.[10]

- In a two year study of incarceration rates, the rates were always higher for high school dropouts regardless of ethnic group. Among male high school graduates, only one in thirty-five young men was in jail or juvenile detention. The figure was one in ten for high school dropouts. For black high school dropouts, one in four was in jail or juvenile hall.[11]

What are some of the issues that make these men feel disempowered?

Many of the young men experience unemployment, homelessness, a dysfunctional foster care system, and the effects of substance abuse. Then there are other issues such as police harassment, incarceration, institutional racism, lack of financial and employment stability, community violence, urban decay,

---

[6] Source: Mortality Tables available at http://www.cdc.gov/men/lcod/2006/BlackMales2006.pdf (last visited on May 18, 2011).
[7] Source: http://www.aclu.org/files/FilesPDFs/collateral_damage.pdf.
[8] Source: http://www.fedcrimlaw.com/visitors/PrisonLore/PrisonEducation2.htm.
[9] Source: http://www.behindthecycle.org/uploads/Beane_Taifa_final.lpr.pdf.
[10] Source: National Bureau of Economic Research website, http://www.nber.org/~kling/494.pdf.
[11] Source: http://www.clms.neu.edu/publication/documents/The_Consequences_of_Dropping_Out_of_High_School.pdf.

racial tensions and gangs, lack of direction, and despair. These circumstances create a sense of hopelessness and despair, which in turn makes them fatalistic.

How does photo-taking help?

When the men took photos, they were looking to share themselves and their experiences through photos. They would reflect on the photos and process the emotions they felt based on the incidences they recounted. Many of the participants had no one they could rely on or trust to hear their stories. Sharing these experiences was a foreign experience for them. So by forcing them to think about the image they were about to snap, the Photovoice Project was able to give the participants something to reflect on, providing an opportunity to think about what they wanted to do and not do with their lives. For example, one participant took a photo of a friend blowing out birthday candles. His reflection on that photo was, "I cried when I turned eighteen because I made it." He was thankful to still be alive; many of his friends died in their teens due to violence.

Then there's a photo of a peanut butter and jelly sandwich with an apple. This was a meal given in prison. Half of the males involved in the project were familiar with what that photo represented. One participant mentioned, "You can get psychologically impaired by the jail system. I went from childhood to adulthood incarcerated."

Another photo depicts a man pushing a shopping cart down an alley. One of the participants said, "This is meaningful for me because here's this man walking down a lonely road without any guidance, and I felt like that in many points in my life, alone and lonely." Another participant described a photo of two Little Leaguers listening to their coach—all three are black—and noted: "You don't really see black men in the neighborhood helping out. But these coaches are giving back to the community. They helped me get to where I am now."

One photo shows two hands put together in prayer. The young man who took it said "God is the only thing that really got me through some of the problems."

What is the background of the participants in the project?

I worked with twelve participants from diverse socio-economic backgrounds. These are some of their stories.

Albert, an Iraq war veteran, was abandoned by his parents when he was four years old. Growing up in Compton, he got involved in a gang but decided to take charge of his life after a bullet grazed his head as a teen. He realized he needed discipline and a life out of Compton. He decided to enroll in the army. This was a way out but he found himself to some extent back in a Compton like environment, with firearms and violence as a common thread.

Justin was brought up in a nuclear family but he dropped out of high school to work as a salesman for a cellular company because "it was good money." He later realized that it was a dead-end job when he noticed that other guys were moving up the chain of command while he remained stagnant. Though he grew up with a father who was trying to help direct him to make responsible decisions, Justin felt that his father was "old school." He could not feel a connection. After all, his father had been a teen years ago—what would he know about being a teenager in this day and age? Justin followed the direction of kids in his neighborhood who were up to no good. He realized later that the direction and advice his father was giving him was the right way to go, albeit too late. Justin now wants to be able to be that role model for younger kids.

JW became homeless as a young teenager when his dad died. He was homeless for about two years while attending high school. He was often harassed by cops at night because he slept in parks. When asked what he was doing there, he would say, "I'm trying to sleep." The police did not believe him when he told them he was homeless and in high school. He felt like everyone was working against him, even the cops who were supposed to protect him.

Logan is of mixed race—father, white; mother, black. He was raised by both parents until his mother passed away in 2005. He was an exceptional athlete who did not care about schoolwork. One season, with a GPA of 1.8, he found himself ineligible to play basketball. He thought of himself as a failure, letting down his mother, teammates and most of all, himself. He refocused his energies on school and became academically eligible to play, but it took him seven years to complete his undergraduate degree with a 2.6 GPA. He became more focused during graduate studies, which he completed in two years with a 3.6 GPA.

EJ was a foster child who sold drugs because it was the only life he knew. He found himself being moved from foster home to foster home. He eventually found a home for over a year with a beloved foster parent but ended up being kicked out because he did not follow the strict guidelines she set forth. That was when he realized he needed to change his ways and direct his path towards education, honest work and making a living. EJ entered transitional housing, worked two jobs while attending school, and slept at work to avoid the long distance commute from home to school. One year after being kicked out of the foster care mother's house, he made amends with her. Shortly after, she died of cancer.

What is the outcome of this project?

In the three years since beginning the project, there has been tremendous change in the participants' lives. The project served as a forum for them to share their thoughts and feelings on different life experiences. Given the depth and richness of their discussions, they quickly formed a brotherhood of sorts. They formed a men's group where they speak to different groups, predominantly young kids, about their experience through some of the photos. They are empowered to make a difference in society and give back to their communities and beyond. EJ is now attending California State University Long Beach. He holds a fulltime job as a security guard and recently bought a condo. He is married and is about to become a father later this year. After joining the project, Albert sought assistance from a therapist to help him with the PTSD from his experience in Iraq. He is now out of treatment and attends Moorehouse College in Atlanta, Georgia, where he is pursuing an undergraduate degree. In the future, he hopes to attend medical school.

Given that you are not black, and that you are Muslim, did the participants look at you differently?

Who says I'm not black? I'm as black as Obama!

This project was initially a project that was set up by my wife and a board consisting of numerous community-based organizations. I served as an assistant to my wife because it was important to make this project a success. I was touched by these young men's stories and ended becoming more and more involved. I think they initially saw me as an assistant and were indifferent to who or what I was. As time progressed, the young men appreciated the fact that I was there. I was told they valued me as a role model—as a husband who is supportive, caring, loving, and committed; as a mentor who advised and encouraged them; and as a human being. Through the process, they learned to trust me and come to me with different issues and see me as a mentor and friend. I hope I helped them realize that they, too, play a vital role in making this world a better place.

What did you learn from this project?

This project started at a very difficult time in my life. I was a new transplant to LA and did not have any friends here. I ruptured my Achilles tendon twice and required three surgeries. I was thankful to be able to do something constructive. As I heard the young men's humbling stories, I realized that something needed to be done. I was motivated. The trajectory of their life course needed redirection and guidance, and I wanted to be a part of that process.

During the project, we found out where these men were coming from. They had a sense of where they wanted to be but had no means of getting there. We helped bridge the gap between the two by forming a men's group where they heard lectures, read materials, and reflected on their lives.

This project helped me contemplate my own values and figure out my place in the world. It helped me realize that I could not be complacent, that

I needed to be active and get involved in social justice—something that the Qur'an teaches. Through this experience, I have formed relationships and friendships that I will have for life.

You are a busy physician. Why was this project important to do?

I grew up in a family where it was emphasized to never forget where we came from. I was fortunate to have a very supportive family and a brother who helped pay for my medical education. He asked that I pay him back by helping others. This was one way I was able to pay him back. More importantly, the Qur'an emphasizes the importance of charity and social justice. That is one theme that I've kept constant in my life—trying to make the quality of my life better through involvement in a variety of causes from childhood education (www.tcsfund.org), this men's group (www.blackmensphotovoice.org), healthcare reform (www.drsforamerica.org), and medical education (teaching medical students and nurse practitioner students at UCLA).

To Sink or Swim

By Yarehk Hernandez

"O My servants, I have forbidden injustice to Myself and I have made it forbidden amongst you. So be not unjust to one another. O My servants, all of you go astray except the one whom I guide. Ask guidance of me, and I shall guide you."
 -First Hadith Qudsi – The Mishkat al-Anwar of Ibn'Arabi
Audhu Billahi myn aShaytani Rajeem - Bismisllahi Rahmani Raheem.

I am a Dominican-American Muslim and an educator. If you hire me, I can fill a few quotas and prove by virtue of being myself that your workforce is diverse. I guess the most interesting part about me is that fact that I'm Muslim at all.

I remember the first time I saw a Muslim. I was a little boy in Brooklyn and my mother and I were walking down a street in Bushwick, Brooklyn. The woman walking towards us wore what amounted to a dark sheet covering most of her body except for her hands and eyes. I was afraid –not because of the woman walking towards us holding hands with her child, but because my mother held my hand tighter and pulled me closer. Like most Americans, my mother knew very little about Muslims at the time and was simply reacting to her own fears of the unknown and the different, but it was this quiet moment spent with my mother that would define the way I interacted with Muslims in the years to come. My education into Islam was birthed on the streets of New York and my curiosity was satiated throughout the five boroughs as I searched for more and more Islam. I studied with the downtown Tribeca hippie Sufis right along with the Upper West Side sober elegant Sufis. All the while searching for an authenticity to the faith that many converts yearn for.

I came to Islam on the streets of New York via Rastafarian weed smoking sessions in Bed Stuy; Kabbalah study groups in City College hallway floors; Hare Krishna vegetarian temple feasts on hungry Sunday afternoons; failed attempts at Tantric Buddhist meditation in posh downtown lofts; and building with the gods in Washington Square Park. My story is not your typical conversion story in which I became enraptured by the call to prayer and recognized the truth of the *deen* and the error of my ways. I guess people want to hear stories like that because they validate their own beliefs in the superiority of Islam, which I can dig if it makes them feel better. My story is not unique but I guess it is not typical either.

I sure as hell don't act like your stereotypical Muslim. I don't wear long flowing robes. I don't have my girlfriend walk tens steps behind me. If I were a "real" Muslim, I wouldn't even have a girlfriend. I'd be married and my wife would wear her *hijab* with pride as she took care of the kids at home, preferably barefoot and pregnant with the next one. I'd be home schooling my daughter as she secretly dated the boy next door. The reality is that I no longer deal with Islam the same way that I did when I began this journey. I guess I'm less dogmatic and strict, but I wouldn't say less pious or less orthodox. Because specific religious communities determine orthodoxy, within my particular blend of American Progressive Islam, I am orthodox. I am the norm and I'm the happier for it. I no longer feel guilt for the things that I do and I am free to love Allah for all that He/She/It brings to my life. I am free to challenge my own prejudices, biases, racist ideas, and homophobia and make myself a better person.

But my relationship with Islam started way before I came to these conclusions. When I started being Muslim, and I choose that word "being" on purpose, I was in college and had come to the end of my tenure as a Rastafarian. My love affair with Rastafari ended amicably. I was never truly accepted into the community because of my light skin, and I don't think I held Haile Selassie I to the same high esteem that some of my Rasta brethren did, not because I didn't think he had been essentially the reincarnation of Jesus Christ, but because I was more inclined to believe that I needed more from my deity. I needed more from God and from my religion than what Rastafari could offer, so I went searching.

At first, I tried looking east, and by east I mean all the Eastern religions popularized by the New Age movement. I went to Buddhist gatherings and learned about meditation, but I couldn't meditate. I then went to some Hare Krishna gatherings, but again couldn't get into all the dancing around and movement that was involved with being a Krishna devotee. I loved the good food good company, though. I still consider some of my Hare Krishna friends dear to my heart and the Bhagavad-Gita a sacred text that has taught me a lot about God and what it means to be a good person. I was a quasi-Rastafarian, soul-searching, hippie wanna-be for a time as I searched for the truth on the streets of New York and opened myself up to what God had to offer me by way of everyday experiences.

I have often told people when asked about my conversion that I came to Islam for a drink of water, but instead found an ocean. The difference being that you can drink from a river or a lake but you can't drink from the ocean. You have to swim in the ocean. The funny part about this metaphor is that I can't swim and am afraid of the ocean's power but the image always made sense to me. I wanted to touch Islam and run away like a kid playing tag with God. I wanted to learn enough about Islam that I could talk about it with a *Jeopardy* sense of trivial authority. Instead I found out that Islam was too vast and closer to my heart than I could have imagined. The first time I picked up *Essential Sufism* and read the opening lines—I was hooked. I felt like I had come home like the dude from Deep Space Nine that blended into the ocean of consciousness that represented his people. The Sufis were my people. Sufi poetry spoke to me directly and, obviously by its popularity in America, to a whole bunch of people. After devouring the whole collection of sayings, stories and Qur'anic verses, I wanted more so I jumped into the Islamic fray.

I started by visiting City College's Muslim Student's Association (MSA). There, a Bengali brother named Nadeem taught me how to pray for the first time, and I found fellowship. The MSA quickly became my home away from home and served the same purpose for many of the brothers who were immigrants to the United States and wanted to practice Islam at school. I would go to the little room in Baskerville Hall and we'd discuss Islam. It was there that I first heard the words *haram* and *bid'a*.

I had come to Islam searching for something deeper than what I had experienced as a Rastafarian and seeking the true love that Sufi mysticism had promised, but learned from my new brothers that what I had read was not true Islam. They convinced me that these sweet talking Sufis with their flowery language had duped me. It was a con. I had been lured to Islam by ecstatic poetry, but real Islam was different. Real Islam was to be learned not from the *shaykhs* and *mullahs* of the world, but from my brothers who were engineering, math, and science majors. They knew what real Islam was because they could think for themselves and could determine what Allah wanted from me and from all of us. They could teach me how to discern the true meaning of Islam by placing in my hands two books, the Holy Qur'an and an abbreviated version of *Sahih al-Bukhari*, one of the most widely accepted collection of *hadith*. Islam was all there inside the Qur'an and *sunnah* of the Prophet Muhammad. Everything else was simply innovation.

The first time I took *shahada*, it was like I was stealing the secret keys to the kingdom or taking some cookies from a jar. I felt like I had a secret to tell and I felt special. When I first converted, other Muslims made me feel like I was on top of the world, but then the barrage of questions, or should I say accusations, began. The problem with "orthodoxy" is that term has been literally hijacked by my extremist coreligionists. It has better funding. We can't compete with the *Wahhabis* and *Salafis* straight up because they have too much money. I see it every day. I have tons of students whose interpretation of Islam is *Salafi*-oriented. They don't know the first thing about their faith because all they hear is the same thing coming from dudes trained in the same places. And believe me—when some dude is preaching with an accent and gently telling me that everything I have ever done is wrong up to my point of conversion—I listened.

I listened because I wanted to know the real Islam and they promised it to me. They were the ultimate gatekeepers into paradise and I wanted in. I wanted to be the best Muslim I could be and these brothers said that they would teach it to me. They would show me what real Islam was and I figured they knew better than me because they were raised as Muslims and came from the magical lands of Islam. The problem with all this was and still remains that the same rhetoric of constriction is used here as it is in Pakistan and everywhere else. These same dudes preach to the poor and uneducated here as they did over there—in Egypt, Bangladesh, Yemen, etc. They rule by good old-fashioned guilt. Muslims born in America are made to feel bad for being American. Americans who convert to Islam are made to feel bad for being American because we all participate willingly or unwillingly in the same American-ness that is that root of what those on the far right in Islamic circles deem to be bad and evil.

Almost every aspect of Western culture is viewed as *haram* and vilified. All I heard as a new convert was "Brother, that is *haram*." My dog was *haram*. My relationship with my girlfriend, whom I loved, was *haram*. My MTV was *haram*. Everything became *haram* to the point that the load was too heavy to carry. Each time I was told that something new was *haram*, or even worse *bid'a*, another straw was added to the heavy load I was already carrying. Islam became a burden to me and it was too much to carry. I couldn't continue to be their kind of Muslim, so I chose not to be anymore.

After living through September 11th in New York, it was easy to fade away from the Muslim community in the City. It felt good to melt back into the pot and be another anonymous Hispanic face walking down Fifth Avenue or riding on the L train. I was just another New Yorker rushing to my next destination. I learned to look away when I saw a fellow Muslim, so that I wouldn't have to give my obligatory "*Salaam*" like I'd been taught and be recognized. I needed to empty my cup of all that I had learned about Islam and relearn what it meant to be Muslim. I had to teach myself, instead of reading books and listening to what others had to say. I learned to define my Islam on my terms and began a second walk through Islam with a renewed interest in making things easy on me. I didn't want a pile of other people's baggage. I wanted to find an indigenous American Islam that allowed me to live the life I wanted to live and still be Muslim. I wanted to own a dog and still love Allah and His/Her/Its messenger. I wanted to hold hands with a pretty girl and not feel like I was going to hell if we stopped and kissed in Union Square for the entire world to see. I wanted to innocently date, listen to music, be friends with girls, shake people's hands, love everyone regardless of religious affiliation, hate no one based on who they loved, and generally be a normal American without feeling like the Devil was my perpetual partner in crime. I wanted to un-*haram* the *haram* and stop hating myself for being me.

Some might say that I gave up, but I like to think of it as liberation. I gave myself the true gift of Islam, freedom. What I have learned, and perhaps what has been the greatest gift of all my years as a Muslim, has been the incredible sense of freedom that purely loving Allah has given me. I get to be Muslim for me and for no one else. "To you be your way, and to me mine." (Qur'an – 109.006) The truth for me was that I had a choice to become Muslim, and beyond the act of choosing my faith, I also had the choice to become this or that kind of Muslim. In my mind, the entire array of Islamic sectarian beliefs was open for me. Although we Muslims believe that humans are born in a state of Islam or submission to our Lord, we understand that the world sways us in this direction or that direction. We are actors in this world who also get acted upon by society, our parents, and our environments, but when we hit puberty or can think for ourselves, the choice to be Muslim becomes our own. Islam, as an act of submission to our deity, is a personal choice. It doesn't belong to someone else. We must decide what we want to be in life and take the necessary steps to achieve our goals. If the same can be said when we make career choices, how much more so when we make choices about how we express our religiosity.

In many ways, expressing the fundamental choices inherent in Islam does not deviate from the party line. Muslims across the board would agree that you have to submit your will to the will of Allah. The divergence comes in the way we express our differences within Dar al-Islam, the Islamic world. When I use this term, I don't mean just the lands where Muslims live, but wherever Muslims are on Earth. We interact with our world, but we do have our own sacred spaces and our own sacred time. We create holiness out of thin air, whenever we stop and pray—whether it be on a dirty New York sidewalk or in Hagia Sophia in Istanbul, now a museum but once a sacred space for Islam and Christianity. The world is our oyster/mosque.

The place where I get in trouble with the "orthodox" *mullahs* is where I say that all Muslims are equal and the same, because Allah makes Muslims. Let me repeat this for those that didn't understand the first time—Allah makes Muslims. Not me, not you, not some *dawa* organization, not the biggest Sufi *shaykh*, not the roughest thug *ulema*, not some NGO working in some Palestinian shantytown, not the *Qawwali* singer, not anyone save Allah (*subhanhu wa ta'alla*). Our Creator lit the match that set off the Big Bang, created the universe over 13 billion years ago, made our tiny little speck of dust 4.5 billion years ago, hurled it through the universe on its axis around our yellow sun, created the primordial soup from which the first proteins where formed—well, I guess you guys get the picture of where I'm going with this.

If my Creator is the creator of all that exists, then He/She/It made me and helped me become the man that I am, which is a Muslim Dominican-American. He/She/It then went on to make you, you and you, too. It's pretty gosh darn amazing considering that many in this creation are so prone to procrastination, like me. And if, Allah makes Muslims and we don't, then He/She/It also makes Hindus, Buddhists, Jews, Christians, Jains, Daoists, and Wiccans. We can share our faith with others through our words and deeds. But it is ultimately up to that piece of Allah's breath inside them to move closer to whatever path motivates them towards a better them. The same is true for Muslims. We follow the way that makes us move our feet.

It's like getting directions. Some people like extremely detailed directions, where each turn is outlined for them and they are deathly afraid of getting lost. Other people just want to get the address so they can go online and let Google do the rest. Other people just want someone to tell them how to get there so that they can share any short cuts they know from traveling. Someone else might just want to punch it all into their navigation system and let the smart sounding voice with the British accent tell them what to do. The destination might be the same, but the way people get there and the choices they make to get there are individual, not to mention the fact that even when you have the directions you can still get lost, or get a flat tire, or hit some traffic on the turnpike, or even worse not get there at all. It's part of the same human story and Islam is just the set of directions I have chosen. I have then added specificity as I have traveled the road. I've learned what neighborhoods I want to avoid, what highways get jammed at certain times, and even a shortcut or two. I went from surrounding myself with stifling "orthodoxy" to setting myself free with Sufism.

Then, I discovered a wide California freeway with people going in many different directions at once within a progressive Islamic vision of orthodoxy. You see, I never knew this until I read the definition, but the community determines what's orthodox and what's not, so within my community of progressive Muslims, we have our own orthodoxy. We hold it to be true that if you call yourself a Muslim, then you are a Muslim. It doesn't matter if you're short like me or tall; black, white or brown; Sunni, Sufi, Shia, Ahmadi, Ismaili or Alevi; gay or straight; male or female; born Muslim or convert; strict or loose; secular or theocratic; or just plain yourself without labels or boundaries. Now I choose to go on the road where everyone can travel and where everyone fits. Even those who won't allow me to travel on their road can come take a cruise on mine because we can all fit.

I remember the story of the Muslims who were shipwrecked on a deserted island. They came across a young woman who helped them with food, water, and shelter. As the Muslims rebuilt their ship, they would stop and perform their daily prayers. When the young woman witnessed the Muslims praying, she inquired about what they were doing. They told her that they were worshiping Allah. After they described what Allah was and the love they had for Him/Her/It, the young woman asked the Muslims to teach her how to pray and practice their religion of Islam. They taught her everything they knew about Allah, prayer, and how to be a good Muslim. Then came the day when the Muslims were ready to leave. They said their goodbyes to the young woman who had helped them, but as they were leaving, she ran to them and asked about the right way to pray once more and they explained it all again. They brought their ship to the water and she ran up to them and asked about the correct *dua* to say before eating, and they explained it again. They reassured her that she knew all that she needed to know to be a good Muslim. She felt confident once again, and the Muslims began to push their boat into the water and row away against the waves.

The young woman waved goodbye as the Muslims began to sail away, when suddenly she remembered that she had forgotten what to say before she went to sleep, and so she ran across the water until she reached the Muslims. As she inquired about the correct *dua* to say before going to sleep, the Muslims' jaws dropped in astonishment because she had walked on water, a miracle attributed to the Prophet Issa. They asked her how she could perform this miracle. She told them that she too loved God but did not have a name or form for Him/Her/It. She said that she would just talk to God and share what she felt from her heart and that God always provided for her. God gave her many gifts including the ability to walk on water. She then asked again about the correct *dua* to recite before sleep. They told her without hesitation to forget everything they had taught her because she had already perfected her Islam.

She had no need for their version of Islam, and neither do we. Islam is here to help us perfect ourselves and no one else. We don't have to prove ourselves to anyone because Allah knows us better than we know ourselves.

Some might say that I have chosen to pick and choose what aspects of my religion I want to follow and leave behind those I think don't fit my life, and they'd be correct if I believed that someone else could determine for me what I held to be orthodox. Allah (*swt*) has given me the right to choose my own way. The Qur'an is my guidebook and the Prophet's *sunnah* my example. The stories of the Sufi *mashaykh* throughout history serve as my examples that time and time again those who choose to follow their hearts cannot be led astray because the human heart is the throne of Allah (*swt*). I can choose not to bully those who disagree with me and instead show compassion. I can choose to support my sisters in their struggle for equality and equity and do the same for my LGBT brothers and sisters, my brothers and sisters of color, and all those caught in the trap of poverty all over the world. My faith demands that I challenge the status quo when it is unfair and defend those who need my assistance. My Islam is one of action and following the *sunnah* of the Prophet Muhammad (*saws*), by doing what is correct and upright and not simply following what someone else has prescribed as the right way to be Muslim. My Islam is a beautiful thing. You should check it out sometime.

The Accidental Fundamentalist

By Ameena Meer

I'm an interesting type of Muslim. The kind you couldn't pick out on the street. There are no obvious outward signs of my faith and my ethnicity isn't clear. You can barely tell I'm of Indian origin because I could pass for Greek, Italian, Spanish, Israeli or even southern French.

The Islam I practice is Sufism—and, in my case, most of my practice is internal. I now call myself a Muslim fundamentalist because I follow what I believe are the "fundamentals" of Islam–generosity, compassion, kindness, loyalty and honesty. I fume at the TV when they call someone blowing up a bus a "fundamentalist Muslim." As someone who lives in downtown Manhattan (and has lived and worked here for twenty years), I hear it a lot. I would call them "nut cases" or "cultural reactionaries," but they could never represent the fundamental essence of Islam.

That's not to say that I don't love ritual, culture, and the joy and magic of tradition, but I believe you have to come to the Divine on your own—and on your own path. As the often-quoted *hadith* (saying) of the Muslim prophet Muhammad (peace be upon him) says, "There are as many paths to the Divine as there are souls."

Sufism is strangely one of the best known—yet unknown—expressions of Islam. Most people know the writings or teachings of Mawlana Jallaluddin Rumi and Shamsuddin Muhammad Hafiz. Their quotes are now on magnets and calendars. I even saw a chic bohemian outfit in the window of the Forever21 store on 34th Street in New York, with a description by a blogger called Rumi.

I have learned
So much from God
That I can no longer
Call myself

A Christian, a Hindu, a Muslim,
A Buddhist, a Jew.
-Shamsuddin Muhammad Hafiz

The idea is that the fundamentals of Islam are almost too great and too universal to be contained in any one religion. Sufism, like Kabbalah in Judaism, deals with the essence of the faith. It includes the idea that the Divine is everywhere, in everything—like the Sanskrit word *Om*, which means the all-encompassing.

Like Buddhism, Sufism is about giving up the ego, the desire for power, the wish to be right, the craving for material satisfaction. These are fundamental concerns of Islam.

For me, this quotation describes the practice of Sufism on a personal level:

Sell your cleverness and buy bewilderment
Knock, and He'll open the door
Vanish, and He'll make you shine like the sun
Fall, and He'll raise you to the heavens
Become nothing, and He'll turn you into everything.
-Mawlana Jallaluddin Rumi

In my understanding of Islamic fundamentalism, the truest practice of faith is demonstrated by our actions on the planet, towards all other life. A brilliant modern thinker in that vein is Ibrahim Abdul-Matin, who wrote *Green Deen*, a powerful Islamic argument, based on Qur'anic quotations, for the necessity of environmental and social responsibility.

Because I'm an everyday single Muslim mother, I go to school on Muslim holidays with my three daughters to talk to their classes. One morning, when my middle daughter was about nine, we were on our way to the *Ramadan* presentation.

"So when do we find out that we're right?" she asked.

"What do you mean?" I replied.

"You know, that Muslims are right and everyone else is wrong. Do we find out when we die?" she asked.

"We're all right," I said. "The goal is to be kind to each other and help each other and find some peace in ourselves. Different religions are just like different languages. It's like calling a chair, *une chaise* in French. It's the same thing. So in Arabic, we use the word *Allah* for God. In French, you say *Dieu*. In Spanish, *Dios*. It doesn't matter what religion you are, you can call God 'Allah,' 'Jesus,' 'Buddha,' 'Shiva'—you can follow your culture—and if you follow something with your heart, you will get to the same place."

Someone once asked me, "How did you, a relatively average, Sunni Muslim American, decide to become a fundamentalist?" It started one *Eid al-Fitr* morning as my older kids, my then-husband, my brother, and I were driving to the 96th Street mosque. The song "What if God Was One of Us?" came on the radio. I started singing along.

"It's sacrilegious to listen to music on the way to prayers," my brother pronounced and turned the radio off. I was in the backseat with the kids and couldn't reach the radio knobs, so my brother got to choose. In one instant, he had turned into one of those judgmental, arms-crossed, head-shaking religious tyrants. I argued with my brother. He eventually admitted that it was the lyrics, not the music, that bothered him.

"There's a *hadith* that says, 'One hour of contemplation is better than a year of worship.' So even if you didn't like the song, if it made you think about the nature of God, it had value," I countered.

Another pivotal moment was a few years later. A young mother was leaving the mosque with two small, squirmy boys and a big stroller. She was stumbling down the stairs, trying to get through the crowd. Since I was too far away to help, I was relieved to see a man hurrying towards her.

"Sister, sister!" he shouted. Instead of helping her, he grabbed her scarf and pulled it back over her head, "Your *hijab* is falling off!"

Of course, there were many more moments. There was the "aunty" in *hijab* who, when asked if she didn't find it hot, retorted, "Not as hot as you'll find it in hell." There was the stand-in *imam* who preached that we would go to hell if we celebrated Christmas or New Year's Eve, said nasty things about Jews and Christians, and explained that it was "those emotional women" who led men astray—thus there were more women than men in hell. I stood up and marched my daughters out past him.

"No one needs to listen to this crap," I said as I walked out.

What I came to realize is what I told my daughter: we are *all* right. If those examples show how those individuals perceive their world, then they need to do what's right for them. However, in my understanding of Islam, imposing restrictions on others based on one's own beliefs risks separating them from their own relationship with the Divine—and no one should do that.

I've been asked how I call myself a Muslim if I don't cover by wearing *hijab*. I respond that, in Islam, being a Muslim requires one simple phrase: "*Ashhadu an la illaha ill Allah, Muhammad a-rasul Allah*," which means "I believe there is no god but God and Muhammad is the messenger of God." This testament of faith implies that you also believe in the Torah and the New Testament. Everything else is between you and God. I have no place judging your choices, your heart, or what calls you.

What I've told my kids is that what you call yourself—Muslim, Christian, Hindu, Jew, Buddhist, Baha'i—is less important than what you do with it. The prescribed practices in Islam are called the five pillars—faith, prayer, fasting, charity, and pilgrimage. I have plenty of friends who are culturally Muslim but in practice are agnostic, never fast, and wouldn't even consider going to Mecca. They drink alcohol, eat pork, and have spent their lives working with underprivileged children in the Delhi slums, helping families in New York City who have been torn apart by the immigration laws, or improving the lives of homeless people. From what I understand of faith, those are the people who are going straight to heaven (without passing through purgatory or what Muslims call "the punishment of the grave")—not the ones who just touch their foreheads to the floor five times a day or starve themselves in Ramadan, while making their families and friends miserable. (Not that one shouldn't pray or fast, but if one just follows the rituals without a spirit of kindness and compassion, one misses the point.)

Again, I tell my daughters that during *Ramadan*, fasting—not eating or drinking—is the easy part. The hard part is abstaining from anger, impatience, and frustration. I tell them that for thirty days, they shouldn't raise their voice, be unkind or hurtful; they should be even more careful not to be untruthful, disloyal, or mean. Trying to do that when you've had nothing to eat and you've been up since the crack of dawn is extremely hard. Many people say that if you get angry when you're fasting, your fast is broken. You might as well eat at that point and start apologizing, because the fundamental goal of fasting is to get closer to the Divine—and how close are you when the small irritations of the material world bring you right back down to the ground?

"Islamophobia"—or the current anger towards Muslims—is something that is part of life for my family. As an Islamic fundamentalist, this is how I deal with it: I act like it doesn't exist. The Muslim Bar Association advocates for Muslims using the civil rights precedents set by the LGBT community—and I follow the example of my gay friends. Like them, I go into every situation assuming that people who don't like me just don't know me yet. I see it as an opportunity for dialogue and a chance to prove religious profiling wrong.

The topic of Islamophobia reminds me of an experience I once had meeting another Indian single mother like myself at a party.

"Don't you hate the way they look at us?" she murmured to me. "The way they are all whispering about us behind our backs?" "Really? They are?" I asked. I'd never thought of that.

Suddenly, the room changed for me. Maybe they *were* all whispering behind my back. Until that moment, I'd always assumed everyone liked me until my actions gave them a reason to change their minds. I'd always thought that my difference was an opportunity to show people that things are never as simple as they expect.

I remember when I first moved to Washington, D.C., just on the edge of my teens, a girl asked me, "Do you like black people?"

I must sound absurdly Pollyanna, but I was baffled by the question. No one had ever asked me if I liked or disliked an entire race of people. Of course, because I was a new kid—brown, Muslim, and Indian, when almost everyone else was white, Jewish or Christian, and European—I was keenly aware of the possibility of getting the answer wrong. Yet I had no idea of what to say.

"I guess there are some I like and some I don't," I mumbled.

That's not to say that prejudice doesn't exist, but as a fundamentalist, it is not to my benefit to internalize it. If I assume that everyone I meet is hostile towards me, then I miss the chance to connect with people who are not. I miss the chance to change people's perceptions. I judge someone's intentions before I experience them.

In the same way, someone who dismisses me without meeting me, misses the chance to find out that a Muslim mother with teenaged daughters is probably spending most of her time thinking about how to get her teenaged daughters to go to Friday prayers instead of watching *Glee*, or how to get them to think more about their schoolwork and spirits and less about their looks.

Not to be Panglossian (as Candide fans will understand to mean "overly optimistic"), but for me, the current public conversation against Islam and American Muslims is a good thing. This spring, while working on social media, I started reading and watching the press about Park51—a planned Muslim community center in Manhattan that has been erroneously dubbed "the Ground Zero mosque."

"Oh my gosh, they all hate us," I said to a non-Muslim friend, "Did I just never notice or is this all new? When did the American public start mistrusting Muslims?"

"No, it was there all along," he said. "It's that no one said it in public."

What happened? It's now socially acceptable to vilify 1.3 billion people (and a faith that has its roots in Christianity and Judaism) in a public forum and even as an election platform. In my mind, that means that Muslims should start addressing the fears and the lack of understanding in a public forum, too. If 60% of Americans say they've never met a Muslim, it's time for us to start shaking hands. We should all be standing on street corners wearing "Ask me, I'm Muslim" badges.

The scary part is that one reason for all this fear and anger is the "Islamophobia industry." As an investigative article in *The Tennessean* points out, keeping the American public angry and on edge generates millions of dollars. Steve Emerson, one popular, self-styled "anti-terrorism expert," makes $3,339,000 a year churning out fear.

To combat the fear, after living through September 11 in lower Manhattan, four other Muslim mothers and I started an organization called Muslims for Peace in November 2001. The project was called 100% Human. My idea was to create a unified Muslim voice for peace—no political agenda—just a million Muslims standing up for peace and compassion across the different Muslim communities. I have friends who wear *niqaab* or beards and I have friends who are gay and lesbian Muslim activists. I even have a friend who's been going on TV and saying she agrees with religious profiling. Yet speaking out for peace is something that we could all agree and come together on. We felt like there were no positive Muslim movements our kids could be part of. One summer afternoon, I had just put my kids on a plane to London and then read in the newspaper about the "liquid bombing plot" just uncovered at Heathrow airport. I don't know the details in the end, but it scared the life out of me. All the Muslims I know are pretty ordinary, peaceful people. I felt like we needed a PR campaign.

Admittedly, the world economy, global warming, and environmental concerns— not to mention, in my case, a mortgage and three girls about to go to college—are scaring everyone. Fear makes people do strange things, which is what I feel is happening in the world today. Whether they are Qur'an burners or soldiers or terrorists, I believe their anger is based on a fear of losing control of life and it represents a way of trying to hold on to something familiar.

Working on the Park51 project—which I have done since its inception—has been an incredible journey into facing and understanding fear, especially fear of the unknown. Much fear is being expressed against the project and against Muslims. What I think outsiders don't realize, though, is that there is just as much fear within the Muslim community. At one informational meeting for the greater Muslim community, a young bearded guy said he'd never come to Park51 because it was full of Sufis, like Imam Feisal Rauf. A man at Friday prayers stood shouting outside one afternoon because *Shia's* and *Sunnis* were praying together. He worried that if the *imam* led the prayers the wrong way, they wouldn't be accepted. A woman was worried she would have to pray too close to men. Another woman was angry at sitting too far away from the *imam*. Some Muslims don't want to go to Park51 because they are worried about men and women, gay and lesbian Muslims praying together. When I was tweeting for Park51, I posted a video from the "It gets better" campaign by a gay Muslim teen.[12] Oz Sultan, the hip Muslim media advisor, alerted the management who asked me to delete it immediately before I offended or frightened away potential funders or congregants.

Many people—Muslim or not—are scared of the government. They are scared of their neighbors. They are scared of change and the future and how it might take away everything that's familiar and move them out of their comfort

---
[12] http://www.itgetsbetter.org/video/entry/wj8zbtcgtja/

zones. Muslims and everyone else are scared of *shari'a* law because no one quite understands what it is. If the Muslims are immigrants or members of a minority, they're scared that the majority will seduce and steal their children away from their culture—a classic immigrant dilemma as exemplified by the plots of "Westside Story" or "My Big Fat Greek Wedding." The future and change might be better. But what we don't know does not make us feel safe—so we don't like it.

That said, this Muslim fundamentalist has been blown away by the level of support we've received at Park51 and as Muslims. It's as if—for many people—the controversy has made them come alive. It has made some question their prejudices and their beliefs as Americans. It has made some remember their experiences as new immigrants. In so many ways, the controversy over Park51 has been a groundbreaking moment—because it has brought the dialogue out into the open.

Recently, I met a guy who is a public relations wiz. When I told him I was involved with Park51, he sent me a video of a TV appearance in which he said the project would never happen. In later emails, he told me that public opinion is against us and growing more hostile every minute (though we might be saved if we hire him). As he saw it, the 9/11 families would never be behind us—yet clearly some are, like 9/11 widow Alissa Torres.[13]

On the ground, what I notice is that when I wear my "One More Muslim for Peace" t-shirt on the street and around the site of the World Trade Center—which is, after all, my neighborhood—people smile at me. They honk from cars. They ask where they can get one. My neighbors ask, "Can I get a 'One More Jew for Peace' t-shirt or a 'One More Friend of a Muslim for Peace' t-shirt?" The greatest impact of 9/11 was felt in the surrounding streets and schools and parks and homes, and my neighbors—Muslim, Jewish, Christian, Hindu, Buddhist, and Atheist—welcome Park51 with open arms. (They especially welcome the planned swimming pool.)

I started making my "One More Muslim for Peace" t-shirts after becoming an accidental fundamentalist. I know there's a demand. As a fundamentalist, I know that, actually, everyone wants peace, harmony and a safe place to live a healthy life.

---

[13] "9/11 Widow: The Media Duped Us," Alissa Torres, available at http://www.salon.com/life/feature/2010/09/07/we_are_not_experts_on_park_51.

I also know that the fundamentals of Islam are the fundamentals of every faith.

The only way to escape from Islamophobia is to click my heels together and say my favorite Dalai Lama quote—the truth we discover as we evolve and the world shrinks and our plastic shopping bags in New York City kill dolphins on the other side of the planet:

"There is no us and them. There is only us."

Regarding the Imp Dancing on the Lintel

By Dizery Salim

IT WAS the summer of 1982—the year I turned seven. I sat in the dining room at Jean Teh's house wondering what to do with my food.

My little sister and I were on a play date at Jean and Lisa's house, whose father, Mr. Teh, worked with ours at the Malaysian Embassy. Tripoli, Libya, would be our home for the next three years.

When it was time for lunch, we sat formally at a big table where Mrs. Teh served us bowls of rice topped with curls of white meat. Maybe I hesitated with my spoon, or did something with my face to show I was less than happy. I don't remember. But she said to me, "Girl, don't be shy. Eat!"

My stomach churned.

Until I was ten, my mother's youngest sister took care of my sister and me. My mother and her siblings called her Ati, and she moved with us as part of our household when my father became chargé d'affaires in Tripoli. Aunty Ati had wavy hair down to the middle of her back. It was she who warned me to watch out for pork at Jean Teh's house. I can laugh at it now, at the notion of finding pork in strictly Islamic and revolutionary Libya, under American embargo. But my seven-year-old self had my aunt's words echoing in my head, "Watch out. They will try to feed you pork." I looked at Mrs. Teh's food and saw poison.

I ate only the rice, which was tasteless and stuck to my throat in unfriendly lumps, so that in time, my bowl became a collection cup for the strips of chicken that I had left untouched. Seeing me, Mrs. Teh began to frown and cluck. "The girl likes to waste!" she said loudly, I think to Mr. Teh, but perhaps to no one in particular. Reaching over, she pinched the leftovers from my bowl with automatic precision. Click-clack. My heart shrank. Click-clack. I heard the message in her chopsticks—I had neither won a point for myself in Islam, nor with Mrs. Teh.

Looking back, I realize my aunt was doing her part to perpetuate my family's brand of Islam. It is what the adults in my family did. But sometimes they took away rather than gave. In one fell swoop, my aunt's words had robbed me of the delight of eating with new friends, when friends were scarce. They had robbed me of nourishment at an age when I needed fuel to grow. They had robbed me of my natural state, that of a living creature that needed to eat as a matter of fact and without guilt.

I think, too, the job of a seven-year-old should be simple: bask in the love of her elders, let them nourish her and tell her that she is perfect as she is, and go to bed happy every night. But I was a Muslim child growing up in an alien world, fumbling in the web woven by the young adults who raised me.

THE CANVAS of my childhood was covered with half-stories of the adults who ran my life, and, over time, I grew accomplished at painting in the gaps. My mother's father—a big, silent man—had a misshapen middle finger on his left hand, which he told me came from a knifing accident. Another time, my mother told me he had injured his hand on the lawn mower. "Or something," she murmured. "I don't know exactly." He knew scores of sacred *doas* by heart and seemed to commune with God while he silently raked leaves under his mangosteen trees in the morning or trimmed his orchid plants at midday, or as he sat still in his armchair on hot afternoons, with his eyes closed.

He and my grandmother kept chickens. Whenever we visited, my grandfather would duck in the chicken coop at dawn and come out with a young cockerel by the neck, the budding cockscomb only just sprouting. The bird would sit in a giant rattan trap by itself while others of its kind roamed freely in the kitchen yard, pecking at insects or darting beneath the flowing vines of betel leaves. After my grandmother had hung the laundry and was ready to cook, he would grab his big knife—so powerful and sharp it could slice open a coconut—and with a swift slash at the neck, kill the chicken in the Muslim way, looking on somberly while the headless animal flip-flopped on the grass.

Once, I tried to get the magic words out of him, the ones that made the meat *halal*. "With your mouth you pronounce *bismillah*," he said. "And in your heart, you state an intention to kill the chicken for the sake of Allah. This makes the meat *halal*."

Bismillah is something Muslims say before doing everything. Roll the dice in a game of Monopoly, you say, *bismillah*. Climb a rickety ladder to hang a picture, you say, *bismillah*. Start your car engine before a long drive, you say, *bismillah*. Several times in my childhood, I saw animals being slaughtered by my grandfather's hand, or by a village headman at the Feast of the Sacrifice or a child's blessing. Each time, I watched carefully to see if I could spot the specific act that made it sacred, the thing that made it different from just rolling dice, climbing a ladder, or starting the car. I never saw a thing.

Still, I had no doubt that God was real and everywhere all at once. The idea was reinforced by Ustaz Osmang, the Qur'an teacher who came to our house once a week in the summer in his polyester trousers and skullcap to teach me *"wau di atas, oo"* (a mnemonic device used to teach us to remember to read the *damma* vowel symbol as [oo]). Aunty Ati would get me ready in my special clothes, *baju kurung*, a boxy, long-sleeved blouse worn over an ankle-length sarong, with an elastic waist for children. My hair was covered in a scarf. With Ustaz Osmang, I would sit cross-legged on the floor of the downstairs study with the door shut, so we could recite at the top of our lungs without disturbing anyone else who was home.

For an hour a week over my school holidays, he taught me the Arabic alphabet, which had six more letters than the Latin one, and showed me how to sound out the letters. Methodically over several weeks, he took me through the reader, the *muqaddam*, the starter kit that all children began with. He taught me how to sound a *mim* at the end of a word when the next word began with a *ba*, and how to recognize when to draw out the *alif* and when to keep it short.

Once he told me, "I teach Arabs, too."

I pictured a Libyan man, scowling as Ustaz Osmang from north Malaysia told him, *wau di atas, oo.*

"You teach Arabs to read Arabic?"

"I teach Arabs the Qur'an, which is sung and not read like a newspaper," he said tartly. "And you sing at the top of your lungs so the devil runs away when he hears you!"

On occasion, our discussions veered away from technique and took a philosophical turn. Once, we talked about God's nature of being able to see everything and everyone all at once.

In my mind, I saw the anthill in the garden where sometimes my sister and I would poke a stick in the entrance hole. Stepping back, we would watch the ants spill out. Hundreds would come crawling out in panic. In those moments, I would single out one ant, watching it scurrying to and fro, grasping a fellow ant on the shoulders and then the next one in line, as if to say, "Are you alright? Are you alright?"

I thought about what the world looked like from where God was sitting. "I'm wondering how God can watch me while watching you at the same time," I mused aloud.

Ustaz Osmang's emphatic answer broke my reverie. "That is the power of God!" he cried, his face triumphant.

I wouldn't call Ustaz Osmang my favourite adult, but in that one instant I thought he was a genius. That nugget stayed with me for a long time: God was not like people. God was different.

ONCE GOD ENTERED my life, I couldn't get rid of God. To my seven-year-old self, God was a certainty. The world was divided into: (1) people who had a God, and (2) people who had a God, but the wrong God. I hadn't conceived of people having no God—I saw only people who were too lazy to put effort into becoming a believer.

"Only people who believe in Allah go to heaven, but we don't tell the non-believers that," I remember my father telling me when I was small.

The divide between Muslims and non-Muslims made for an awkward situation. I belong to the second generation of post-colonial Malays. The first generation included my parents and their cohorts, whose batch of prep school graduates went on to solidify Malay political power in a power-sharing arrangement with the Chinese and Indians. The Malays were Muslim, while the Chinese and Indians were not. After independence from Britain, Islam became the state religion of Malaysia even though it was not everyone's religion.

When I was five or six, my family went to a Christmas party given by the neighbors who lived on the street behind ours on Jalan Terasek. They were an Indian family.

Their house had an identical layout to ours. There were presents under a plastic fir tree next to the staircase, which stood where our staircase stood. The tree had been decorated with tinsel, like in the photographs from my children's books. The Indian family was very nice to me and gave me a striped candy cane to suck on while the adults made conversation. It was curious to me that, of those adults, some would go to heaven (my parents) but some would not (the Indian neighbours). But I accepted that it was true and tried to learn about hell as much as possible. I knew it was a place where people were tortured alive and I hoped it wasn't so bad, for their sakes.

FOR AUNTY ATI, God was a trickster, and the practical jokes had mostly to do with pigs.

She was the one who told me to watch out for pork at the Tehs' house. The year before, when I moved from kindergarten to big-kid school, Aunty Ati was also the one who told me that, sometimes, ice-cream filling in creamsicles was made from pig's milk. She told me to watch out especially for the creamsicles sold by Chinese sellers on their motorbikes outside school gates.

My mother did nothing to dissuade either my aunt or me of this notion. But creamsicles were so good, I was past caring. For weeks, I had been gobbling them on the way home from school without breathing a word to the adults. One afternoon, while savoring a creamsicle after school, the whole thing slid off the wooden stick and landed on my school pinafore. It caused a huge stain on the blue cloth. As I walked into our house, I held a schoolbook over the stain to keep it from view. My mother and aunt were in the sitting room, observing me. "What are you hiding? Remove that book," said my aunt. I did so, and seeing the mess, she demanded to know what I had spilled there. I kept silent.

Years later, my mother settled the issue. One day, she came home from the school where she taught, declaring that one of the other teachers—a Chinese man—had told her that people were as likely to drink pig's milk as dog's milk. But until then, whenever I ate a creamsicle, I never forgot that I would have to account for it in my grave. As they take turns questioning me, one of the two angels of the tomb will ask: "Dizery Hadijah Salim, is it not true that you consumed creamsicles that may have contained pig's milk?"

AFTER WE HAD been in Libya for a while, the Tehs left and were replaced by the Gopalas, an Indian family. Just after the Gopalas arrived, my parents threw a dinner party for the Tripoli diplomatic corps and Mr. Gopala, in his exuberance, hung *wau bulans* on the stair landing. There were usually no children allowed at dinner parties, but my parents were rebels on that score. As we dressed up for the night, Aunty Ati gave my fingernails a dark red polish and I put on my blue summer dress and my blue ankle boots with a fringe. My sister and I had matching boots, which the adults bought for us in London where we had just spent two weeks.

When my father saw me, he looked angry, but I wasn't sure why. All my life, my father would become enraged over small matters, which he never allowed me to forget and made me carry around like a neck iron for months at a time. Once, when my sister was three, we were squabbling over who owned a leather pencil case. My father ended the fight by taking the object and flinging it out my bedroom window. Both my mother and Aunty Ati called him crazy, and Aunty Ati made me go outside to fetch the case. Shaken by it all, it was some minutes before I made it down three stories, out the door and to the area of the garden underneath my window. When I got there, I saw that Sidi, the new groundskeeper from Ghana, was raking the gravel and pellets of sheep's poo that he used as fertilizer, his face frozen like a mask.

My heart was in my mouth. "Did you see a pencil case come flying out that window?" I demanded nervously and a little impetuously.

"I saw nothing," Sidi told me, leaving me to scan the ground by myself. I did not find the leather case. Later, I learned he had four children of his own. I wouldn't be surprised if he took the pencil case for himself to give to his kids, with thirteen colored pencils—and a pencil sharpener—inside. But at the time, I trusted him implicitly. After all, he was Muslim.

The night of the dinner party, I thought maybe the lipstick had set my father off, but I couldn't tell. Over the school holidays, I would consume tube after tube of Smarties, smearing the red ones across my lips to stain them with food coloring in a parody of lipstick. Seeing me, my father would tell me lipstick was made from animal placenta and wasn't something I should be wearing. I heard this from him again and again in my childhood. Each time, I turned the thought over and over in my mind, never quite figuring out what made it wrong. Maybe the placentas came from pigs, just like Aunty Ati thought creamsicle filling sometimes came from pig's milk.

Or maybe my father—a ritualistic man who became a *haji* in his mid-thirties, which is earlier than most—disapproved of the nail polish I was wearing. You had to be able to wash off all your make-up before you said your prayers and anything permanent, like tattoos or nail polish, could nullify a prayer because it stained you.

To me, this rule was a certainty. I believed in its truth. When I spied my Arabic teacher's nails, which were shiny-red and encrusted with rhinestones, I blurted, "You can't pray with nail polish on."

"Of course you can," she said, her kohl-lined eyes narrowing into slits. I was unconvinced.

I never did discover what caused my father's displeasure that night. As he went about inspecting the table settings—at thirty-two years of age, already showing signs of a micro-manager in the making—he said to me, "I know who did this to you. Wipe it off. And I want to see you put on some proper shoes, please."

AS A CHILD, I was a frequent vehicle for my father's loud religious statements. At the Oil Company School in Libya, he used me to fight the American institution of Halloween. My first year at school, he announced on the day of the Halloween parade that I was not permitted to wear fancy dress like the other children, because Halloween had a Christian connection and was a spiritual threat to my Muslimhood.

For my part, I saw no threat. Even as a child, I understood that no other person's myth could harm my essence as a Muslim. At age eight, I knew my father's pronouncement had nothing to do with protecting me, and instead had everything to do with resentment he harbored against a world whose default was Christianity: school was closed for Christmas and Easter; we sang psalms at the school concert: "Michael, row your boat ashore, hallelujah."

I don't know if my father understood that I was acutely aware of the difference between me and my non-Muslim friends. But at eight years old, I was at a loss to describe my difference, especially to my teachers and friends.

What was left to me was to brave each Halloween as best I could, wearing my normal clothes while my friends delighted in their wild headdresses and flowing skirts, or danced around in feathers and face-paint. Watching them, I was stoic. Inside I was crushed to be the only child not able to dress up like my favorite cartoon character, or a cat with whiskers, or a one-eyed pirate, and never to be in the running for the best costume award.

RETURNING TO MALAYSIA from Libya, my parents sent me to the British school where the ex-pats sent their kids because my Malay was too poor for me to succeed in Malaysia's public schools. My sister attended a Malay kindergarten and primary school, where she had no problems with religion. But the spectre of religion would hover over me like the plague.

My parents had written to the school to request that I be excused from Bible lessons. While the class whipped out their Bibles, I sat silently at my desk and opened my novel. The one or two other Malay students in my class took Bible lessons like the other students because their parents had planned to send them to English boarding schools and Scripture was an entrance exam subject.

Mrs. Lee, not my favorite teacher, took me aside one day and said, "Why are your parents so narrow-minded?"

I was hurt. I reported the comment back to my father, but it only strengthened his resolve to keep up his personal war with the rest of the world.

Even though I sat out of Bible studies for a year, I followed with stealthy interest the scholarly explanations of the difference between the Gospels of Luke and John, of the significance of the rivalry between Jacob and Esau, and of how Joseph rose to power under the seven years of lean. Only a few months later, when my family moved to Los Angeles, California, my parents made the decision to enroll me in a Catholic all-girls school because friends had recommended against sending me to the public school system in our district. At Immaculate Heart High School, I sat through mandatory Bible classes three times a week, drawing on what I had learned at British school. I even memorized passages in a contest once, though I didn't win. I did everything short of going to mass and accepting communion.

SO, WHERE does this take me? The concept of God is not something you can convey in one sentence, but for the adults in my family, when raising a child to believe in God, one-sentence descriptions were the way to go. In this, my family was extremely consistent. The end-result was that religion was passed down from adult to child in my family in learning episodes where the lessons were so brief that I had no room to linger and ask questions: Why were some people Muslim and not others? Were they born that way, or was it a choice? Why couldn't I eat what I wanted?

One night in Libya, when I was seven, I was unable to sleep. My sister was asleep next door in my aunt's room. The house was quiet. I had lain awake in the bedroom, staring at the shape made by the chandelier. My gaze went to the outline of the door, which the adults left slightly ajar to let in light from the stair landing. As I lay there, I thought I saw an imp dancing on the lintel. It was the imp from hell, I told myself, taunting me for not doing things right. I was Muslim, but I had feelings that wouldn't mold themselves to Islam.

The aunts on my father's side wear *hijab*, while the ones on my mother's side do not. "Islam is easy" is a popular chorus of my *hijab*-wearing aunts, a butchering of a famous saying of the Prophet, "Allah does not want to place you in difficulty." But I never found Islam to be easy, not as a child, nor as an adult. For me, Islam is difficult in a world that is not Muslim.

The Me Monologues

By Mona Eltahawy

How do you discuss virginity with a class of American university students without the conversation sounding irrelevant to their lives or, worse, an exercise in exoticizing another culture?

Women, sex and culture can be a Bermuda Triangle that threatens to demolish discussion through either defensiveness—when students feel compelled to defend a cultural practice—or superiority—when students feel compelled to parade their culture as being above whatever cultural challenges are being discussed.

The personal is not only political but it demolishes that Bermuda Triangle. I got a powerful reminder about that in September when I taught a course on gender and new media in the Middle East, in Oklahoma. We had watched the Lebanese film "Caramel," directed by and starring Nadine Labaki, as the owner of a Beirut hair salon whose friends and coworkers portray a cross-section of Lebanese female experience.

One friend undergoes hymen reconstruction just before her wedding to a man she fears will reject her if he finds out she isn't a virgin. Students didn't miss a beat.

"Have you heard of purity balls?" asked one young woman, referring to formal dances in the United States between fathers and daughters at which teenage girls pledge to remain virgins until marriage.

I thought, Yes! It was an especially sharp class. Most of them were majoring in Women's and Gender Studies. They were comfortable with the personal and with making those connections. I had indeed heard of purity balls through news articles, but they seemed to be as foreign to me and to the class as hymen reconstruction.

Until the personal shook us out of our complacency. "I just want everyone to know that I signed a purity pledge with my father," one of the students said.

I could not have engineered it better myself. Her courage in sharing reminded us all that virginity wasn't just over there in Lebanon. It was right in class with us. Oklahoma kept doing that to me. I joke that going there was like going to the Middle East: a similar mix of religion and conservative politics. (Oklahoma is the only state in which every county was red after the 2008 presidential election.)

Some of the other students tip-toed toward questions for the student who had shared her purity pledge experience. We were all adjusting.

"I respect that you think you've made a free choice," one student told her. "But [playwright] Eve Ensler said that when you sign a pledge to your father, your sexuality is being taken away from you until you sign it to your husband when you get married."

Teaching is like alchemy. You take a few students, mix them with some difficult subjects and you are bound to be stunned by the results.

I make my classes as personal as possible. I offer my experiences to keep a face on the issue we're talking about, and so the least I could do to appreciate the generous sharing we had all witnessed—and to express solidarity with a conservative position I once shared—was to tell the class how long I had waited to have sex. There were no purity pledges in my past. But there was a time when I, too, believed I should wait till I got married before I had sex—but then it took forever to get married and I got fed up waiting.

When I was younger, I had no one to share that with. The guilt was exacerbated by secrecy and for a long time I could talk about sex only with non-Muslim women friends.

But I've become bolder. It's not always reciprocated or appreciated. At one Muslim women's conference, after I shared how difficult it had been to overcome the guilt of premarital sex, another Muslim woman bluntly told me that the Qur'an clearly stated that "fornicators were for fornicators," so there was a "fornicator" out there for me somewhere.

Charming.

Undeterred, sometimes driven by an insatiable need to share—share and shed the guilt—my skin has thickened. It was made more resilient in Oklahoma—so familiar that some evenings, alone in my hotel room, weeping was the only way to let go of memories, some as far back as twenty years, but still close to the bone.

Oklahoma prepared me well for Amsterdam. Differences in moral ethos aside, my reward for all that sharing with my students was a group of Dutch Muslim women of Moroccan descent with whom I could talk honestly about sex—safely and without any self-righteous references to "fornicators."

"When I first had sex, it was as if my mother, my father, my grandparents, the entire neighborhood, God, and all the angels were there watching," one of them said. The rest of us convulsed with laughter and all too familiar memories.

Male-dominated religions and cultures that cater to male sexuality, with barely a nod to women's desires, are difficult enough without the judgments of fellow women. I know where it comes from; I recognize its need to conform. And like our virginity discussion, the best way to defang the self-righteousness is with the personal.

Women's stories are too often dismissed. A male editor I once worked with tried to dissuade me from the personal: "Who cares about what happened to you?"

The most subversive thing a woman can do is talk about her life as if it really mattered.

It does.

Reprinted from *Jerusalem Report*, January 3, 2011

My Teacher

By Ismail Butera

Personal dignity and integrity are the hallmark of a spiritually content being. Long ago, I learned this from a spiritual man who taught that faith is not only a belief in God, from whom all goodness and peace emanate, but a reflection of that belief as manifested in our individual dignity and honesty to each other as human beings. What I absorbed years ago guides me to this day. My experience reflects the vital role our spiritual community leaders must play in setting life examples and planting the seeds of spiritual knowledge, understanding, and tolerance.

Ever since the fateful events of 9/11, many Muslims like myself, born and bred in the West, are viewed with scrutiny. This sad day will be remembered not only for the violent deaths of nearly three thousand innocent people, but also as a turning point in relations between communities, friends and acquaintances. Opinions were formed and old wounds and prejudices reopened. Until today, violent attacks against innocent civilians by suicidal terrorists validate the notion that Islam is not a religion of peace. There is also a general feeling that many "moderate" Muslims, though not bad people, are not vocal enough in denouncing terrorism and call to re-establish the caliphate and implement *shari'a* law. Many in the West remain mistrustful of Muslims, even bestowing upon the English language a new term: Islamophobia.

The mistrust of Islam and Muslims in the West is old, as Christianity and Islam have historically and politically been at competitive odds. The rise of a new and violent Islamism, sometimes called jihadism, has reopened a can of worms. Osama Bin Laden and his partners successfully transported us back to a time when East stood against West and hate and bigotry ruled the day. We are at the threshold of a rift that does not seem as if it can be mended as members of various communities seek to insult one another with a near medieval ignorance. People of all faiths who like to believe that we live in an open-minded twenty-first century are alarmed by burning religious texts, vandalizing mosques, and murdering innocents in retaliation to perceived insults. It is as if Muslims, Christians, and Jews, all monotheists, held nothing ethical or moral in common. As though we worshipped different gods and disavowed each other's claim to Abraham's teachings. As if symbiotic interfaith work had never been attempted at all. East is East and West is West…the twain never met and never will. Is this how far we have come? There must be another version of the story.

In fact, it wasn't always like that. Muslims have been a part of the American scene for a long time. Everybody knew about boxer Muhammad Ali who said that according to his faith it was wrong for him to fight in Vietnam. Americans in the twentieth century knew the famous so-called "Syrian peddler" who visited their houses once a week and sold dry goods. Most of these peddlers were Arab Christians, immigrants fleeing intolerant Muslim rule, but some were impoverished Muslims, especially in the Midwest. They were good, hard-working people. So were the thousands who worked in factories during World War Two, building tanks and airplanes to help the United States fight fascism. Muslims were everywhere: the guy in the candy store, the owner of the family-run diner or coffee shop, the cab driver, the doctor, the accountant, the pizza man, and the peanut vendor on Broadway.

Muslim kids went to the same schools as everybody else. Some did well in math and some played hooky; they hung out with friends, went to church with them, and attended their *bar mitzvahs*. They dated and went to after-school dances. The Muslim mosques were small, and kept a low profile, but Muslim families were open and hospitable to their neighbors. They ate steak, drank too much coffee, and ordered pizza on Friday night. Some drank a couple of beers and some had two cars in the driveway. Grandparents may have quietly mourned when their Muslim child married a Catholic and brought their kids up as hippie flower children in the 1960s. For those who were really into it, there were spiritual teachers who preached a benign and inclusive Islam such as Hazrat Inayat Khan or Bawa Muhayadeen. Or one could read Idries Shah and learn *The Way of the Sufi*. The occasional vitriol from certain Muslim leaders was not taken by Americans to be mainstream. They were branded by Muslims and non-Muslims alike as lunatics. Back in those days, in the 1960s and '70s, most non-Muslims didn't roll their eyes when they heard that Islam meant submission to the way of peace.

Some of the kids descended from Muslim immigrants wanted to look back and investigate their less-known Muslim heritage. After all, Muslims were not here in the United States in great numbers, and the story of their presence was not as widely known as that of other groups, such as European Christians. These young people had vivid memories of a praying grandparent, an uncle who didn't eat or drink at certain times, or an aunt who ate the chicken and coleslaw at a barbeque but passed on the hot dogs, at least until she had read the ingredients on the package to make sure no pork was involved.

These memories posed deep questions for many young Muslim Americans, myself included. Who am I? Why am I here? What are my roots? For me, those questions were coupled with the desire for personal spirituality, a relationship with the eternal. I was ready to embark on a quest for the meaning of life itself. This is how I came to know the practice and wisdom of Islam.

Mine was not a very religious family, so it was a solo trip all the way. I searched and investigated. I read, studied comparative religion, and prayed for guidance as best I knew. As a young musician, an accordionist interested in ethnic music, my connections to the Albanian community brought me in touch with immigrants from that mountainous Balkan land. Albanian culture prides itself on ancient music, symbolic folk dances, and proud traditions such as bardic storytelling. Performing and attending the community's parties and celebrations, I was amazed at the calm religious tolerance and unity of these passionate and temperamental people. Catholic and Orthodox priests regularly attended the gatherings and picnics held by *Sunni* Muslims or members of the Bektashi Sufi community. I could see there was a kind of inner harmony among these people who were outwardly secular and rather non-religious. "*Zoti eshte nji misteri emathe.*" God is a great mystery, I was told repeatedly.

Albanians are reluctantly religious at best. Albania, being a poor country, didn't have prestigious schools of Islamic theology. Indeed, many *hodjas* would attain their formal higher education at a Catholic Jesuit university, like the one in the Albanian city of Shkoder. Islam was a folk affair and it was learned on a local level. There were moderate-sized *madrasas* in Sarajevo, Prishtina and Skopje—located in Bosnia, Kosovo, and Macedonia, respectively—where one could travel to get some instruction, but no big schools comparable to those found in the Middle East. Maybe this was a good thing since, with their troubled history, the last thing Albanians needed was dogmatic religious scholars to ignite conflict and complicate already tense political matters. Perhaps it was the Albanian tradition of seeing diversity of faith as part of the mystery of God, combined with their negative historical experience of conquerors who used religion to divide and subdue the people, that gave birth to their culture of religious tolerance.

My prayers for spiritual guidance were finally answered in the form of a simple Albanian man from the small town of Diber, in the very heart of the Balkans. He was the *imam* of the local Albanian American mosque, a small and unimpressive building in a run-down part of town, and was fairly well known among the Albanian Muslim community in New York City. He showed up one day for a casual visit while I was at the house of a dear friend, a relative of his. Over strong Turkish coffee, served black in tiny cups, my friend told the imam about my desire to learn more about the Islamic faith. The *hodja*, as *imams* are called in the Balkans and Turkey, was delighted that this young American was so interested in his own heritage. He was impressed that I had taken the time to learn so many Albanian folk songs and melodies, as well as the language itself, which I was busy expanding beyond the few Albanian words and expressions I had learned as a child from my mother. He cheerfully agreed to teach me what he could about Islam: how to pray, fast, recite passages from the Qur'an, explain and study *hadiths*. All after Friday prayers. Like the study of music or language, I would need patience and discipline to learn the faith properly. I felt that if what I was reading in books about Islam was demonstrated to me in practice and principle, I could then apply those principles to my own life correctly. I needed a living example. *Hodja* was that example.

A simple shoemaker by trade, like my own Albanian grandfather, *Hodja* was a prince in the realm of wisdom and social tolerance. He hadn't learned Islam at the prestigious schools of Islamic learning, and he didn't speak colloquial Arabic. However, he had learned to read classical Arabic and thus could recite and understand the Qur'an. As a young man, *Hodja* had escaped first from communist Albania, and then from Yugoslavia, where he faced discrimination because of his Albanian ethnicity. After that, he spent some years in a refugee camp in Italy. Throughout his life he met and interacted with people from many ethnic and religious backgrounds, and willingly worked at any occupation to make ends meet. These experiences during his travels, as well as the ecumenical traditions he grew up with in his homeland, helped to foster a very understanding and open-minded man.

Far from the stereotypical tales of bloodthirsty fanatical horsemen with curved sabers, I found that Islam was a viable and complete system for life. I learned that it advocated tolerance and compassion for all beings, acknowledging the faiths that came historically before it. Islam demands that a Muslim be a good citizen rather than a distant observer or non-involved participant in society. Islam is not at all about being an outsider, but rather about being very much on the 'inside' and actively a part of one's community. All this I learned from *Hodja*.

Learning sometimes can be a shock, an unexpected event that rocks your ego and your soul at the same time. What *Hodja* taught and demonstrated to me about Islam overwhelmed me with joy and gratitude. I developed a faith that answered my innermost questions and set my heart at ease. Finding myself, or, if you will, being discovered by God, was like finding a diamond in the sand. Logical reasons for this are hard to explain, but when it happened, everything seemingly fell into place. I embraced a faith that put me in a one-to-one relationship with my creator, yet allowed me to function in the modern world as I always had.

I felt a desire to display that inner transformation, to outwardly manifest my sheer delight. I purchased a Muslim cap to wear to prayer and a necklace with a gold crescent and star emblem on a black shiny background. However, I was to learn that symbolism can get in the way of real spirituality.

"What is this?" *Hodja* asked me directly when I went for my weekly religious lesson.

I explained.

He shook his head from side to side and said in his accented English, "No, no good. Not for you."

Needless to say, I was puzzled. I asked for an explanation.

He patiently explained, mostly in Albanian, that a Muslim need not manifest his faith in his dress, but rather through his good deeds and works.

"One should dress as the people in one's country dress. Do not try to look exotic or different," he told me. "This brings attention to yourself and can be a way of showing off. It can give you a sense of superiority over others. Pride is of the devil: *haram*."

He explained that standing out from others also can bring down the wrath of one's society, making one the identifiable scapegoat. Indeed, *Hodja* himself always dressed in a smart suit and wore only a beret when he prayed. He looked like anybody else. No beard, no sandals, no robes. No signs that said, "Look at me, I'm Muslim." Non-Muslims knew him as the "Albanian priest" or the "Moslem minister."

Naturally, I discarded my necklace. I didn't wear the cap again either. Instead, I donated it to the mosque, where it went into a bin that held such caps, similar to the bin that holds *yarmulkes* in a Reform Jewish synagogue. Most worshippers take one when they enter the mosque and remove it when they are finished praying. God doesn't need us to make a show of His faith outside the doors of the sanctuary.

Hodja manifested his faith and devotion to Islamic principles by extending those very noble principles to neighbors and non-Muslim friends. I was pleased to learn that he rented out a storefront in the building he owned to an African-American Baptist church. Some people in the Muslim community questioned this, but he calmly explained that the church was a house for the remembrance of God, and that this was something that God would like very much.

"It is important to satisfy God first, not people", he always said "though it's easier to love God than to love people."

Hmm... Was this an example of that famous Balkan cynicism? Maybe.

"Only if God thinks it's wrong, will I ask the Baptist minister to leave," *Hodja* said.

Obviously, God didn't complain about a Christian church rented out by a Muslim *imam*.

Hodja would visit the Baptist minister on Sunday after services, and the two men would share coffee, conversation and spiritual points of view. I learned from that experience that in the desire to satisfy God, you do satisfy people.

There seems to be an opposite pattern going on today, with some members of Muslim communities demonstrating antipathy towards many basic foundations of pluralistic American society. A number of Muslim religious leaders tend to invoke a spirit of standing outside the American dream, defending all things "culturally" Islamic such as *niqab* and traditional forms of dress, social restrictions on women and children and implementation of *shari'a*, which they insist supersedes any civil law. These same Muslims utilize democracy's pluralistic ideals when it benefits their cultural identity.

I believe this is hypocritical and clearly wrong. It stands against the true spirit of Islam that I learned from *Hodja*. Today's self-imposed culturally-distanced Muslims living in the West, pushing their agendas and their beliefs onto Muslims and non-Muslims are creating a rift between communities and inviting bigots like the Qur'an-burning "Pastor" Jones to do their stuff. What happened to the example of Muhammad's Medina, where different groups of people lived side by side? What about regard for the "People of the Book," their rights and feelings? I was taught that it is incumbent upon Muslims to respect others and do what one can to get along with them. We wear the dignity of our faith on our persons. Honesty and good intentions are of prime importance in society, especially in a pluralistic society.

At the end of the fasting month of *Ramazan*, the local mosque was traditionally cleaned and polished, making ready for the *Bajram* holiday (also called *Eid al-Fitr*)—and an American flag was hung outside the mosque. The congregational prayer of that day would bring nearly everyone to the mosque, people from many different ethnic communities. Along with these different communities, however, came different concerns and outward manifestations of what exactly Islam is supposed to be. The very secular minded Albanians are very conscious of separating religion and politics, but other Muslim peoples may not be. One year, on the eve of *Bajram*, a group of men at the mosque challenged *Hodja's* decision to display the American flag, something he had done every year.

America was the place where *Hodja* had finally found complete freedom of religion and conscience. In his view, guided by the teaching of his faith, a Muslim is commanded by God to uphold the country's honor by respecting it. For him, placing a flag outside on this important Islamic holiday meant that his congregation was loyal to the ideals of democracy and the government of the United States. It was a way of showing that Muslims are thankful for the opportunity to practice their faith freely and without hindrance. This gesture was meant to build bonds and bridges between Muslims and other Americans.

The group of men, whom I would now identify as *neo-Salafis*, complained about the flag and threatened to tell people in their ethnic communities not to attend the *masjid* of those who "willingly turn a blind eye to the sufferings of the Palestinians and other Muslims around the globe due to the acts of the Americans and their Zionist allies."

Needless to say, *Hodja* would not wait for the next day's sermon to expound on the importance of the Muslim community to always behave honorably and demonstrate their respect. To illustrate this point, he recounted the story of the early, persecuted tiny group of Muslims whom Muhammad sent across the Red Sea to seek protection with the Christian king of Abyssinia (present-day Ethiopia). *Hodja* related Muhammad's words in Albanian. I can still feel the electricity in the room as I translated the tale into English, word for word: "In Abyssinia lives a good Christian king, who follows the teachings of the Gospels of Jesus. No man is wronged in his country. Go there and seek the protection of this rightly guided ruler."

In this incident from early Islamic history, the pagan Meccan ambassadors who went after the Muslim refugees demanded that the small group be returned to Mecca to be tried and punished. The wise king, however, decided to question the group. He asked what their prophet Muhammad said about Jesus Christ. They related the story of his miraculous birth to the Virgin Mary as it is revealed in the Qur'an. They told the king who they were, what principles they followed, and what they believed in. The king, moved by their story and their dedication to their faith, drew a line in the sand with his staff.

"The difference between you and us is no greater than this line," the king said. "Stay in Abyssinia as long as you wish."

Muslims hold that the good Christian king of Abyssinia saved Islam from imminent doom, to the chagrin of the pagan Meccans who were out to destroy it.

Through this story, *Hodja* explained to all present that it is indeed the Muslims' responsibility to appreciate and respect the country that protects them.

"If it was good enough for Muhammad and the early persecuted Muslims," he said in conclusion, "it's good enough for those of us living today. The American flag remains and will fly proudly outside the mosque during the feast of *Eid al-Fitr*."

He ended with an emphatic "Finito!" (He was quite fluent in Italian, too.)

Islam as a religion places no burdens upon its believers. It is amazingly adaptable and is meant to exist in any cultural surrounding. There are Muslims in places as far afield as China, Senegal, and the Ukraine, places with different climates and cultures. However, the *Wahhabization* of Islam, the forced implementation of ancient desert customs upon what is supposed to be a universal faith is causing massive problems for Muslim communities. The faith that was intended to liberate humans from clerics and religious tyrants risks becoming clerical and tyrannical. Instead of having a one-on-one relationship with God, exercising their personal intellect and reason, Muslims are told by other men how to approach God and how to think and act towards other humans. Rather than quoting the beautiful verses from the Qur'an or edifying examples from Muhammad's life, many *imams* and *mullahs* take a more negative approach to faith.

Why? One reason could be that some Muslims feel they are better than everyone else since they possess the final revelation. However, as *Hodja* once told me, being God's *khalifa* is not the same as being a Pharaoh or a Nimrod. Pride should not dictate to us the rules of coexistence. Recognizing God's word and power in everything around us is the true sign of an enlightened soul. That is what we should strive for, not the separation of God-consciousness from His magnificent creation. Nor should we succumb to tyranny.

I can never forget what I learned from this simple but incredible man. He was conservative and strictly adhered to his faith. He believed in a "live and let live" policy, because "to God, we shall all return." I don't think *Hodja* would approve of the push going on these days for the acceptance of the *niqab* or the implementation of *shari'a* when secular democracy defends anything that a Muslim would need in any legal situation. *Hodja* never complained or moaned about being discriminated against. He knew all about discrimination but also knew that God doesn't discriminate, so discrimination becomes a moot point. I learned from him that there is no God but God, and no life but this one and the one to follow. That means you must live this one life as best you can and not create any unnecessary trials for yourself or others. *Hodja* taught me to remember the final goal: to live with dignity and manifest that dignity for God's sake. Everything else comes naturally.

His powerful personality and sense of will inspire me to this day. Forbearance and patience in the face of life's trials, humbleness in demeanor but swiftness in acting against a wrong and defending the right, mercy and compassion as the greatest forms of charity; these are teachings to live a good life by. In my work today as a storyteller and music therapist, I reach out to young and old and seek to build bridges and bonds among diverse communities of people. All of us, regardless of our background, have similar criteria for what is right and wrong, just as we all agree on what is hot or cold. "We are," *Hodja* said, "after all, a human family".

After the breakup of communism, *Hodja* returned to the land of his birth and passed away peacefully, in his late nineties. I still have the hardcover A. Yusuf Ali translation of the Qur'an that he gave to me years ago. I am thankful for this man's wisdom and teaching, and his patience with a young fellow who asked endless questions in rough Albanian. Through his actions and deeds, he demonstrated to many people what it is to be a Muslim in society, as he defined it clearly and without doubt. We need leaders like *Hodja* today, to define Islam and stand for its ethics and virtues, by acting responsibly, building bridges across communities, and demonstrating the tolerance and compassion that are the very cornerstones of our faith.

Peace, oh *Hodja*.

Allah Loves Us All

By Shahla Khan Salter

Allah.

The word echoes in my heart. It has always been there. He has always been there.

I have no memory of when I heard the word *Allah* for the first time.

It was likely the hour I was born and my father whispered the *azaan*, or call to prayer in my ear.

But my earliest recollection was hearing it from my mother as a child. It was a summer night and a warm breeze blew through the window as I lay in my bed. My mother said it—softly—over and over, until I fell asleep, her hand gently patting my back—"*Allah, Allah, Allah, Allah...*"

My sisters and I—her babies—heard it every night until we were old enough to fall asleep on our own. "May Allah protect my children and keep them safe from harm," she whispered in her native Urdu and then, before she rose from our beds, she blew softly onto our heads, symbolically blowing her prayers upon us.

It was as though she blew from her heart all the love in her soul onto us.

Allah. The word filled me with calm and made me feel safe.

But not everyone believed in Allah I learned as I grew up in the seventies in my hometown of Winnipeg. When I was six years old, my friend's family found out we didn't celebrate Christmas. At their home on a play date, standing beside a Christmas tree, questions were asked.

"What are you?" asked my friend's older sister.

"Pakistani, Indian," I replied.

"What religion?" she asked.

"Muslim," I replied.

"What's that? What do you believe in? God?"

"Yeah. We call Him Allah," I said. I said it shyly. I pronounced it like my South Asian parents with two long a's—"*Ah-lah*." But my non-Muslim friends didn't say it the same way nor did their parents. It was always "*Aaaa -laaa*" with two short a's.

For some reason, the way they said it—at the time—made me feel alien, though in every other way, I was a regular kid, hanging out in the neighbourhood with my non-Muslim friends, where we rode our bikes, played tag, and travelled freely to one another's homes.

But I still knew I didn't fit in entirely anywhere else outside home - except for one place. There was one place where no one would ask questions about why I didn't eat pepperoni pizza, or celebrate Christmas, or read the Bible, or why we prayed on the floor to "*Aaaa-laaaa*."

And that place was my local mosque.

At the time, it was a special place. My dad and many of my parents' friends helped to build it. I will never forget the first day I entered. My mother drove us there, excited, telling us in the car how it was almost finished. When we arrived we were surprised to find my dad, a physician, who was not very handy at home, on a ladder, hammering nails.

It was a small mosque with one entrance. The Muslim architect, a family friend, who designed it had two daughters, a son, and a spiritual outlook on Islam. He made it with one door to welcome all. He made it with one prayer hall for all of us to pray together. Men were to pray at the front and women at the back—but women could enter through the front door comfortably and walk to the back of the prayer hall, in plain view of the men.

I recall walking into the prayer hall through the front door with my mother. I recall seeing my mother, young and beautiful then, walk unimpeded past the men in the prayer hall, quietly, often staying on one side, ensuring not to disrupt anyone's prayer by moving in front of him or her. When it was time to go, my mother directed all of us to the front, where my father was gathering with the other men, and talked to him easily, as she could anywhere else.

And as our community grew, the space between men and women, in the prayer hall, from the front to the back, narrowed, but no one ever seemed to complain. On *Eid*, when the prayer hall was packed, both genders congregated not only in the main prayer hall, but also in the basement, together.

And when the women in the back could not hear the *imam* at the front, they spoke out right then and there, insisting he speak up. Out of respect, the volume on the microphone was immediately turned up.

The mosque became the place where our community gathered—not only the South Asian community, but all Muslims in Winnipeg, from all over the world.

It was a place not only where my mother could take me and my sisters to study Arabic and learn about Islam, but where my sisters and I could sit comfortably among our brothers in Islam—our peers—without barriers, right beside them. We could speak out, asking questions and making comments during our lessons and be taken seriously. It was a place that formed us, shaped who we were and who we would become.

At that mosque I met other kids—boys and girls—who were Muslim, who avoided pepperoni on their pizzas, who sometimes felt bad about not celebrating Christmas, but in turn asked for special gifts on *Eid*, and whose parents taught all of us that we were lucky to live in Canada.

Then, in the eighties, our world changed.

I was in my early teens when Muslim countries such as Iran, Pakistan, and others were declaring themselves to be Islamic states, and governments were imposing what they considered to be strict *shari'ah* law.

The *Mujahideen* were fighting the Soviets in Afghanistan and were admired for their courage. Oil rich Saudis were travelling the world, leaving in their midst rigid interpretations of our holy scriptures.

Soon that interpretation colonized virtually every mosque in the West.

And suddenly, our mosque changed. The rules changed. The atmosphere changed. Now there were two entrances—the original front door reserved for men, and fire exit in the back for women.

Soon there was a partition to separate men and women in the main prayer hall.

The partition and back entrance were supposed to stop women from being seen entering and leaving the prayer hall.

If you looked through the grates of the partition, other women closed them, sometimes abruptly. If you were a woman, you could no longer speak in the prayer hall loud enough for men to hear you. Comments and questions to the *imam* from the back of the prayer hall stopped, and no longer could a girl or a woman greet a friend—or even her father—who happened to be seated on the other side of the partition.

If you were a boy or a man, you could not turn around and see your sisters in Islam. You could no longer meet the friendly gaze of your female friends, or even your aunt.

It was unlike anything I had ever known.

We were told that it was to protect us—not just girls. Our brothers were told it was to protect them from what could happen if they mixed with us. But I refused to accept that Allah condoned such isolation even under the guise of protection. I refused to accept that I needed protection from my "uncles" and my male friends and the brothers who were seated next to my father in the front of the mosque.

After all, wasn't I safer entering through the front main entrance than the fire exit at the back? Wasn't I safer walking through the front door of my mosque—the one my father helped build—alongside my brothers in Islam? Wasn't I safer here than anywhere else because it was my mosque?

At the same time, no longer could I attend the mosque without wearing the *hijab*. Normally I only wore it to pray, out of respect and humility for Him, not for any other reason. Now if I did not wear it before setting foot on the premises, I was subjected, at minimum, to a few disapproving looks from female worshippers who wore it regularly, at worst, to warnings from men whom I did not know.

And these men did not say the word, *Allah*, the way I had said it my whole life. They did not say it softly. They said it loudly, with emphasis on the second syllable, "*al-LAH*". They said it angrily, I assumed because their *al-LAH* did not approve of the way I dressed, or the way I looked them in the eye, or the way I asked questions challenging their rigid views of Islam.

It made me angry. The foundation of my faith, the way I perceived Allah as loving and merciful, differed from theirs. Was I an interloper? Was I not a true Muslim? Was a true Muslim only one who wore Muslim clothes as defined by these men, one who did not question the meaning of the rules they said defined our faith? Was a true Muslim someone who performed all the rites and rituals of Islam out of fear of a vengeful *al-LAH*?

I watched as grown-ups in our Muslim community, who taught me about the beauty, justice and humanity of Islam, said little or nothing or simply left the mosque.

And then, as though He willed it, the brilliant spectrum of colours and influences from all the communities surrounding me emerged.

My best friend in high school was Jewish. She said the word *Aaaa-laaa* with two short a's, but it made no difference to me because together we marvelled at the commonalities of our faiths. She taught me that the Hebrew word "shalom" like "salaam" not only meant peace, but that the full greeting was "shalom aleikhem".

She told me how her constant questions during Hebrew lessons angered her religious teacher so much, her parents were forced to find her another one. She told me she had promised her dying grandmother that she would marry a Jew. We laughed as she wondered aloud if she would ever marry. She knew I could relate as I wondered aloud, when my perfect knight in shining armour came along, would he be a Muslim?

At this time, some of the girls in our Muslim community in Winnipeg donned the *hijab*. For virtually all of them, it was a choice. For some it was out of modesty. For others it was a rejection of a society that exploited a woman's beauty for commercial gain. For many it was about confirming their Muslim identity.

For all, the decision was made from the belief that according to Islam the *hijab* was required to be worn by Muslim women.

A divergence of ideology separated us. I found my closest friendships formed with those whose heads remained uncovered and whose faith was apparent not by their manner of dress but by their words and actions alone.

Even so, our "*hijab* friends" were still our friends and our sisters in Islam. After all, as children we had played together many times and still shared memories from Islamic summer camp. A piece of cloth did not change their hopes and dreams—ones we all shared—to go to school, to build a career, to fall in love and marry, to live happily ever after.

Some of them started to pronounce the word *Allah* the way the men transforming the mosque had said it. But their hearts did not hold that same anger, and, like me, they had many questions for them.

From the diversity around me, I continued to encounter an inundation of thoughts and ideas that crossed cultural and faith lines. Looking back, I will never forget my former law school classmates—Christians, Jews and Atheists, who expressed outrage at the civilian casualties during the bombing of Baghdad in the first Gulf war. Nor will I forget, soon after, the Muslim "brother", who performed the *khutbah*, at our university Friday prayers and swore that our greatest enemies were the Jews. I will never forget my Muslim "aunties" and "uncles"—my parents' friends, my friends' parents—who completed the village that raised us all, showing how men and women respect one another and build life-long friendships. Nor will I forget the English teacher, born in North America like me, who said she assumed I was not really Canadian and so did not understand the material and graded me accordingly. From all of them and many more, I learned that love and anger do not discriminate regardless of faith. No, love and anger arise out of all of us no matter how we pronounce the word "*Allah*" and whether or not we believe in Him.

Now, I live in Ottawa, Canada's capital. It is post 9/11. I am a lawyer by profession, married and the mother of three children. I have seen how the status of a woman is elevated or denigrated by the laws of her society, and what this means to her family, including but not limited to her father, husband, brother and her son. I have a husband who respects me and shares my values that the true message of faith is about justice, respect, humanity and acceptance. We pass along this message to our children. We teach them Islam at home. We work to show them that we are its ambassadors by endeavouring to share our values of peace, justice and humanity with others.

Surfing the internet one night I search the word "Muslims". There it appears—"Muslims for Progressive Values". I click and the words "God loves Beauty" appear and reverberate through my psyche. Scrolling down fast—the principles of equality and justice that are declared reflect my already held core values and beliefs. 'Out loud—they said it,' I think. These are my fearless brothers and sisters in Islam. They are not afraid to declare the principles that are based on the one premise I hold most dearly in my heart: Allah loves us all.

But my journey does not end here.

It is August, 2010, Ramadan. Called "Islamists," terrorist suspects have just been arrested by our RCMP. They make the headlines of our local and national news every day. Police state that they believe the suspects planned to blow up targets in Ottawa, where numerous Canadians could have been injured and killed.

My fellow Canadians are shocked, most intensely by the fact that some of the suspects were born and raised in Canada—"homegrown," according to police. Regularly in the paper Ottawans express concerns about their security amidst their Muslim neighbours. My fellow Muslim Canadians rush to the media to defend the integrity of our whole community.

But this is not enough and never will be.

Words that do not translate into action are meaningless in the face of not only the terrorists who hijacked our faith but as well the seeds of intolerance that inhabit our mosques. Soon, I will tell our local paper and by doing so, all of Ottawa, that the only way to prevent the radicalization of our Muslim youth is to arm them with a love for all of humanity.

And so it is only one week following the arrests that I march with the first Muslim contingent at Ottawa's Capital Pride Parade.

There are only four of us including R. Ahmed, an openly gay Muslim university student who leads our contingent. We wear shirts that say "Muslims for Progressive Values" on the front and "Allah loves us all" on the back in big letters. We carry a banner with the same words. Throngs of people gather on either side of the street. They smile and clap as we make our way down Wellington Street, past Parliament Hill.

I hand out brochures for MPV. I see a young woman in *hijab*, standing in the middle of the crowd. I go to her and hand her a brochure. She thanks me. As I make my way back to my contingent an elderly man chuckles and says, "Where is *Aaaaa - lah* now?"

And out of the crowd, a man, young and white, replies, "He is everywhere." It takes my breath away.

I return to my contingent. We have made our way down Wellington and we are about to turn the corner onto Elgin Street. The crowd increases exponentially at this corner.

Shahla Khan Salter   135

Suddenly we are in a wide open space. Our banner is more visible than ever. The contingent of the United Church immediately in front of us is suddenly further up ahead. The Unitarians, who had followed us, are suddenly further behind.

We are a small group of Muslims, on our own, with a message for our city: "ALLAH LOVES US ALL".

The crowd bursts into cheers.

The War on the Home Front:
A Queer Muslim Family after 9/11

By Tynan Power

"We're at war!" my mother screamed into the phone. "Turn the television on!"

That morning of September 11th, the urgency in my mother's voice moved me to action. I had to switch the TV on—CNN was the background music of my mother's life, but I usually got my news online or from the daily paper—and caught the second plane hitting the World Trade Center, live. I had no idea what was happening. Those planes, they were our own commercial jets, not enemy fighters, yet my mother was screaming "war." If this was a war, it was like none I'd ever learned about in history class.

I ran back and forth from the TV to my computer, trying to get news as fast as it came. Quickly, the identities of the hijackers became part of the story spreading like wildfire: first their names, then later nineteen images laid out like a card game, one face after another with dark hair, dark eyes, skin of varying shades of brown.

"I have to get Yahya out of school," I realized, panic rising in my chest, forcing out all the air in my lungs.

Yahya, my firstborn, half-Arab son with beautiful Mediterranean coloring, was already a proud young Muslim at age ten. Our family's faith was no secret, but it was even more of a popular topic for him at the start of every school year, when he talked incessantly about his summers with family overseas.

The new school year in Massachusetts had just started a few days before September 11th. That year, Yahya was starting middle school—lots of new kids, plus the big change from elementary school. His preteen sixth-grade awkwardness read like a bold Sharpie "kick-me" sign on his back already. He didn't need another reason for peers to target him. I rushed to get to him before his multi-cultural chatterbox landed him in more social trouble than his Arabic name was going to elicit.

For my younger son I could breathe a sigh of relief. I knew his name would bring no attention to him, and most of his peers and teachers at the elementary school didn't realize he was Muslim at all. The only clue they generally had was that he didn't eat school lunches containing pork—as a result, to our amusement, everyone seemed to assume he was Jewish.

Within minutes, I was in the office of Yahya's middle school. We didn't even have to explain why I was there. The vice principal immediately tried to reassure me.

"We're not telling the students what happened. We think they need to hear it from their parents. Their parents will be able to help them understand what happened and deal with their emotions. So right now, they don't know. Everything is fine. And once they go home today…well, you need to know that we will not tolerate any bullying, any slurs, here."

The sixth-graders spent that day in a warped cocoon at school, their innocent ignorance broken by occasional rumors passed around by students who had somehow gotten the news already. When he got home, Yahya knew something had happened but didn't know exactly what. Someone dropped bombs on New York? Someone crashed a plane? Was it in New York? Washington? Did someone blow up the White House?

Four planes, four crashes, three locations, nineteen perpetrators, thousands of casualties—it was too much for a ten-year-old to put together from rumors. Even after telling the story as I knew it, it didn't make much sense. I explained again, trying to get it right. But what was right?

Even for adults, it was too much to make sense of in those early days. We were all asking ourselves the same questions. What were the motivations? Who organized it? What country was behind it? Was there a country behind it, at all? Would it happen again? Were we all at risk?

Answers were slow to reveal themselves. One thing that was clear quickly was that the terrorists were Muslims and that Al-Qaeda, in taking responsibility for the violence, had claimed to be acting in the name of Islam.

"But Islam doesn't allow killing innocent people," Yahya said, his brow furrowed.

The notion that Muslims flew planes into buildings to kill people who were going about their everyday lives conflicted with everything Yahya had learned about Islam. This "Islam" that promoted violence was not the Islam Yahya learned at home, in his summers with family overseas, at the mosque, or at the Islamic school he had attended for a few years. It made no sense to him just as it made no sense to me.

What I needed, desperately, was to talk with other Muslims—particularly Muslim parents. Yet during that time I felt increasingly isolated.

As a queer, transgender Muslim, I had traded in my conservative Muslim community in the South for a life of being more true to myself as an out queer writer and activist in Massachusetts. Since 1998, I had been part of a rich, diverse community of queer Muslims online and then through Al-Fatiha, an LGBTQ Muslim organization. Serving on Al-Fatiha's initial *shura*, or advisory board, I helped the organization focus on various goals and projects—including offering support to LGBTQ Muslims and educating others about queer and transgender Muslims.

The founder of Al-Fatiha, a young man named Faisal Alam, was invited to speak all over the world. Doing so, he risked his safety again and again, defying threats made against him personally and against Al-Fatiha, collectively. Part of me wanted to be right behind him, backing him up and ready to step up when he needed to step back. I vividly recall that the first time we met, I made a commitment to him to do just that as often as I possibly could.

Yet as a single parent at the time, I had to be cautious for the sake of my children. I carefully weighed my risks when speaking in public. Still, there were many times when I spoke at conferences and events about queer or transgender Muslim issues, such as when Faisal and I were keynote speakers at the 1999 True Spirit Conference for transgender FTMs. Coupled with the burgeoning of the queer Muslim movement with Al-Fatiha at its epicenter, these experiences helped me build a broad network of queer Muslims and allies. It was that network that I called "my community," despite how geographically scattered it was.

In my city in Massachusetts, I had a different kind of community of politically and socially progressive queer people, none of whom were parents—or Muslim. I had friendly acquaintances among the parents of my children's friends, yet none of them were queer—or Muslim. And then I had my community of queer Muslims, none of whom were nearby—or parents.

My family loved Yahya (and for the most part they didn't share the popular bias against Muslims that was starting to run rampant), but they felt strongly that I shouldn't have given him an Arabic name, shouldn't have moved to the country where he was born in the first place, and shouldn't have converted to Islam.

It would have been nice if all the shoulds I'd violated in my family and faith of origin had earned me a new community of people who shared my experiences, but they didn't. What I lacked was precisely what a local Muslim community could have provided: support as I wrestled with how September 11th and the ensuing wars in Afghanistan and Iraq were affecting my children; local Muslim friends with whom to share concerns over coffee; for my children, peers facing similar name-calling and prejudice; and maybe most importantly the opportunity to stand shoulder to shoulder in prayer with my Muslim brothers and sisters, seeking a more transcendent resolution to our earthly disquiet.

Yet, for me, as a queer Muslim, the local Muslim community did not feel welcoming or safe. Though no one in the local mosque had threatened me or challenged my presence, I was all too aware of anonymous threats against Faisal and Al-Fatiha members, including me. As someone who once identified as a conservative Sunni, I was well aware of the deep-seated homophobia and inexplicable *transphobia* in many Muslim communities. While most conservative and traditional Muslim religious leaders have historically held that homosexuality is not permitted by Islam, contemporary high level religious authorities of the major branches of Islam have affirmed the validity of the transgender experience and the rights of transgender Muslims to transition. This fact is widely ignored by lesser Muslim leaders. Subjecting myself to judgment and condemnation at the mosque, and potentially subjecting my sons to more bullying because of our queer family, would not bring the support I needed.

Our identities grew more fractured. In queer community, I didn't talk about Islam. Among queer Muslims, I didn't talk about my family. At school, my children talked less and less about Islam and our family's observances of Muslim holidays. I didn't talk to my non-Muslim family of origin about how anti-Muslim bias was affecting us, and they, in turn, remained oblivious. I wrestled alone with how to inform my children about the realities of bias and prejudice, as well as war and terrorism. What I did most was listen.

On September 11th, some of Yahya's classmates had, in fact, gone home to parents who could help them understand what happened and who were able to listen to their fears. Some went home to empty houses where they found out about the attacks by turning on the TV. Over the next few weeks, virtually all of the children in America witnessed replays of the planes flying into the World Trade Center, over and over again. Televisions were always on. Twenty-four-hour news channels told the same stories over and over, because they couldn't talk about anything else and there was precious little news to report: so few rescues, far too few survivors, endless despair of helping those trapped in the rubble, so much terrible death. Everyone seemed to slide into a collective state of PTSD.

The middle school brought in a psychologist to talk to parents about how to help their children. She pleaded with them to turn off the televisions. Repeating graphic images of violence retraumatizes viewers' minds, especially children's minds, she explained.

"If you have to watch the news, watch it when the kids are in bed, or when they're at school, or in another room, at least," we were told. Yet that was so much easier said than done. It's nearly impossible to control how much TV children are exposed to outside the home—like at Grandma's, where CNN was turned on before the coffeepot every morning.

Even in my house, where the TV was rarely on, there were times over the next few months when we would watch the news together. Yahya wanted to know what was going on. Both planes that crashed into the World Trade Center had taken off from an airport he himself had just flown into days before. His community was in a state of collective shock and grief. His country was under attack and would soon declare itself at war with two Muslim nations. The United States seemed to be at war with Muslims long before the official wars began. Some might say the war began before 2001—perhaps even that the West had never really stopped fighting the Crusades—but for American Muslims there was no longer any doubt after September 11th. Public enemy number one was Muslim.

Every time someone on television said "Muslim terrorists" it ran together as one word: "Muzlemterrists," like a pop star whose full name is slurred on the tips of rushing teen tongues, the "Britnyspears" of political pundits everywhere.

Some tried to create some breathing room between Islam and terrorists acting in the name of Islam, using words like "Islamists" and "jihadists" to differentiate between extremists and average Muslims. The semantic ploy won some rounds—the words remained in popular usage in 2011—but lost many, including accuracy. "Islamists" may believe in a political system based on Islam, but they are not by definition militant. The term "jihadist" is even more perplexing. The term is based on the Arabic word *jihad* that means "striving" and usually is used by Muslims to mean "striving for God"—the greatest example, as the Prophet Muhammad said, being the *jihad al-nafsi*, the striving of the soul towards God, no swords (or bombs) involved.

"Muzlemterrists," meanwhile, remained the mainstay of the news networks long enough for it to make its way into the vocabulary of every Walmart shopper in America. For Yahya, in the school that "would tolerate no bullying," there were also the phrases "Bin Laden lover" and "dirty Arab" with which to contend. Every day, there was one hallway to pass through where a neighborhood boy would tell Yahya to kill himself.

It was hard for me to know when to complain to the school. I could have gone in every day for a year with a different plea to help my child feel safe in class, between classes, at lunch and on his way home. The suicide prompts definitely got me an appointment with the school administration. Less vicious things always had to be weighed against how much more torment he'd endure for having gotten a bully "in trouble."

There were no easy answers. The school did what it could. One child was moved off Yahya's bus. Others were reprimanded by teachers, served detentions, and no doubt dealt with parents who had been called in for a conversation with the school. I was never sure if I was demanding too much or not enough.

When I looked at Yahya then, it never seemed to be enough. When I look at him now, I know that it was enough in the most important way: he survived.

Eventually, in fact, he thrived. In high school, Yahya channeled his "multi-cultural chatterbox" into being a "spokes-Muslim." Every semester, he was a guest lecturer in a world history class, as it covered an Islam unit. He arrived each time wearing layers of t-shirts with Islamic slogans—like "Muslims Do

It 5 Times a Day!"—which he'd peel off, one by one, as he moved through his topics. He was invited to a middle school in another town to give his guest lecture to seventh-graders there. At a local Unitarian Universalist congregation, Yahya helped teach a seventh-grade class about Islam for a semester and, together, we led a worship service sharing our understanding of Islam as a progressive, inclusive faith.

Somehow, he found the patience to bear with constant scrutiny from airport Transportation Security Administration workers, as he flew back and forth to visit his family overseas. As soon as they read his name, they would immediately mark his ticket and wave him to a special line. While it enraged me to see my child—as young as eleven—being "randomly selected" every single time he went through security, he took it in stride and answered the questions of towering adults with badges more calmly than I could have. Ordered back from the security line when I tried to keep a watch on what was happening to my underage child, I seethed.

"When did this become a country that picks on children?" I wondered. Where could I complain when the bully was an agent of the government?

For Yahya, it soon seemed like it had always been that way. Was there a time before racial profiling? Not in his memory. Away from the airport, Yahya wore his Hijabman t-shirt that read "My name causes national security alerts. What does yours do?" with a good sense of humor that spread to those around him. That humor, ultimately, may have been his saving grace.

My family—like many Muslim families in America—has evolved to cope with the fallout of September 11th. Like non-Muslims, we mourned the attacks on our country, but then we also grieved the attacks on our faith.

The face of Islam in America has been evolving, too, as progressive Muslims organize to make themselves heard over the voices of extremism, mainstream mosques open their doors to interfaith gatherings, and even the traditionalist Islamic Society of North America talks about bringing Muslims together in all their diversity.

I've had to re-integrate the pieces of my life that became disjointed after September 11th: family, faith, queer identity, and local community. To me, that has been a profound *jihad*. Bringing my faith into the queer community, where Islamophobia is often rampant and unchecked, is no picnic. Bringing my queer self and feminist values into the Muslim community is often an even greater struggle in the path of God. Striving to keep my own faith strong in the face of so many challenges—my *jihad al-nafsi*—is, definitely, as the Prophet said, the greatest struggle of all. Yet engaging in these struggles actively means my life feels less fractured, my energy is less segmented, and the work I'm doing in my communities—all of them—feels more vital and more hopeful.

As with any evolution, I can't know what lies ahead, but I do know that there is only one direction I can move: forward—in the path of God, in the path of integrity, and in the path of peace.

Islam at Needle Point

By Nakia Jackson

Islam is firmly knit into the fabric of Philadelphia's black community, and most Philadelphian black families, including my own, have Muslim members. My parents, however, demonstrated that spirituality isn't an end product but a process, and the result was a mix of Judaism, Christianity, Islam, and agnosticism. Divide that between two parents, and that makes for some rather confusing holidays. Growing up, I knew exactly what I wanted—the firm faith of my Muslim family, friends, and classmates. My spirituality would not be a messy process; I would do it properly.

I knit my Islam with stitches that were perfect, stitches that allowed no room for slackness or unevenness. Philadelphia's African American Muslim community is filled with men and women whose faith is clad in virtually bulletproof certainty, and I wanted, needed, *had* to be one of them. I got the most traditional yarn, the most authentic needles, and I followed the instructions of the books to the letter. I wanted to follow the pattern of the life of the Prophet and his companions as exactly as humanly possible, so I knit my Islam with the wrist-straining tension of the beginner.

For about five years, I knit my Islam so tight, there was no room for doubt. Or at least I tried to. Upon the advice of people with beards and clothing that clashed with their surroundings, I came to believe that the more out of touch I was with creation, the more in touch I was with the Creator. To be removed from twentieth-century America was to be connected to God. I long to be connected with God, and I wanted it then with a zeal that missed the forest for the trees. I wore yards of polyester, parroted Arabic phrases that I didn't bother to look up because they sounded Muslimy enough, prayed all the prayers, fasted all the fasts, didn't shake men's hands. Yet I was morally bankrupt. I was creating a garment shaped by hatred for those who were different from me. I participated in boycotts of Jewish-owned companies because I somehow thought that it would change the course of a conflict that no one around me understood. I viewed myself as superior to non-Muslims, to Muslims who didn't wear *hijab*, and to gay, lesbian, bisexual, and transgendered people of all faiths. And of course, my Islam had no ease or softness for anyone struggling with an addiction. I was so obsessed with perfection that I forgot that Islam is about creating beauty. I had knit myself a garment of moral ugliness, self-hate, and bigotry in every technically perfect row. But I kept knitting, as I was afraid to consider the consequences of being wrong. Being wrong meant hell fire. It meant alienation in this world and punishment in the next. I feared being in error on a point of *fiqh* (Islamic jurisprudence) as one might fear a wild animal. It made me abandon what I loved in order to seek safety with those who had to be right, as they spent so much time telling me that they were.

As my life furled out before me, I kept spotting signs that the Islam I was knitting wasn't going to look anything like what I'd hoped. It soon became very hard to reconcile myself to statements such as: "The man has to be in charge; that's the way of al-Islam," or "Non-Muslims are misguided; Muslims should be running things."

It became increasingly difficult to defend these notions to those interested in Islam. This difficulty sometimes stemmed from the logical holes in the position, but even glossing over those started to leave me feeling tainted, as I was coming to see the moral failings that I was promoting in the name of morality. Muslim women who expressed contempt for women who didn't wear *hijab* seemed alien and intimidating to me, even though just a year before, I would have echoed their condemnations. I could either continue in denial, fashioning an ugly, misshapen sense of my place in the world, or I was going to have to make some serious corrections.

Every knitter faces this point at some time in his knitting career; to have to rip back to continue knitting after a grave error. I don't know if every Muslim has to do the same. One night, I sat, took a deep breath, and began to pull at the ideas I'd formed about myself, my place in creation, and the value of other human beings. I needed to rip out heteronormativity as my moral stance, the vaunted superiority of those who come from traditionally Muslim areas. I needed to stop measuring piety in yards of polyester, and re-knit my Muslim self-understanding with the wisdom I had gained and a love of humanity as God's creation as my guide. I began to ask questions about the assumptions that many Muslims make about the role of Muslims in the world. What would a God who created us all equal think of the hierarchies we've established and the exploitation and oppression that we visit upon one another?

Since that night, I've come to reject and be ashamed of the ideas I held about Islam and knitting when my stitches were too tight and my ideas much too simplistic. Most of the time, I'm in a conscious struggle to change my thinking. At other times, I realize that I never believed what I was told in the first place. There are areas that seem impossible to rip back, like my views on *hijab*, and others that seem to unravel with barely a touch, such as homophobia. There are ideas that I'm ripping out by the fistful, such as anti-Semitism, and ideas that I need to delicately tug at, like my views on the Israeli-Palestinian conflict. In the process, I've gotten the support of friends, family, and total strangers who consoled me when I needed it and challenged me when I deserved it.

My transformation has not been entirely smooth; I've had feelings of deep regret over things I've said and faced accusations of attempting to "destroy Islam." I've lost friends and probably killed my marriage prospects. I've been threatened for my stance on women's rights. I've become "unmosqued." When people ask me who "my *imam*" is, or where "my mosque" is, I can but shrug, or perhaps direct them to the works of people like Imam Feisal Abdul Rauf, Omid Safi, and Khaled Abou El Fadl. I wanted my son to grow up in the mosque, but that seems well-nigh impossible without moral compromise. But the friends and faith I have are truer and more sustainable. What I've lost in zeal and convenience, I've gained in grace and authenticity.

So, I've got a pile of faith that looks kind of shaggy. I've got contradictions and undeveloped ideas all over the place. Please don't ask me too many questions about exactly why I think women's leadership matters, why love is more important than technical perfection, or why I think that vacuuming the mosque carpet is of greater value than most sermons. I'm a traditionalist at times, but I throw tradition to the wind at others. My tension isn't even; I get tangled up sometimes, and it's definitely slower going this time around. But the fabric of my life, as it grows, is soft, strong, and offers warmth to others. I cannot knit the same Islam that the Prophet wore. It wouldn't fit in any case. But I can stitch together a living example of Divine Mercy.

My Story:
An Interview with El-Farouk Khaki

By Afdhere Jama

Since the early 1990s, El-Farouk Khaki has been a pioneer. He formed the first support group for gay and lesbian Muslims in Canada. He called it Salaam, offering a peaceful solution to an issue that haunted many before him: how exactly do we reconcile our sexuality and our faith? Later, he would become a respected immigration attorney, defending the rights of gay and lesbian refugees in his country. And in recent years, he has run for political office. But whether he is running a campaign or leading a prayer, something that is always present in El-Farouk's life is his undying support for the equality of all people.

Afdhere Jama: Something people don't imagine when they first meet you is that you were born in Tanzania.

El-Farouk Khaki: Because to be "African" you apparently must be black. Or white. It is interesting that white people's nationalities are never questioned. A Chinese Canadian who is a fifth-generation Canadian is still asked, "Where do you come from—originally?"

I know. It is one of those things about being a minority in the West. Do you consider yourself African?

Yes. I am a queer African Muslim man of color, a feminist and an immigrant. I am brown skinned from Black Africa and was born into a small Muslim community in Tanzania that has been traditionally marginalized by the mainstream.

Do you have memories of Africa?

I was seven when we left. Yes, I have some memories. I have bits of memory—of Dar es Salaam and Nairobi, which is where my mum and I stayed after fleeing Tanzania and before we got to England. My bits include family, school, sitting on my grandmother's lap, or listening to my grandpa tell me stories. He was good at telling stories. I have bits from a trip to Bagamoyo, the old German capital of Tanzania, and going to the beach after *fajr*, as the fishermen were bringing in their catches and selling them on the spot. I recall listening to my mum on the phone with my dad, telling him to remain in London while she found a way for her and me to get out of Tanzania. I also remember going on safari with my aunt Dolly, her now late husband Mohamed Amin, and my baby cousin Salim.

Why did your family leave Africa?

My family fled Tanzania in 1971 to escape political and religious persecution. In many parts of Africa that were under British colonial rule, you had to be Christian to get an education. That is why even in majority-Muslim countries, the educated and political elite is Christian. The same was true in Tanzania, where Muslims were at least equal in number to the Christian population. My father was part of the independence movement. After independence we had "one party democracy," which means we had a dictatorship. Hence after independence, the repression of people who were potentially "problematic" for the regime. My father fit into that category, so we had to leave.

Where did your family flee to?

After we had all left Africa, we spent three years in the United Kingdom, essentially without status. Then, my parents secured permanent residence papers for Canada. We landed in Toronto in March 1974 to find two feet of snow. In Tanzania my father had been involved in the Experiment in International Living, an organization that brought Westerners to Africa and gave them homestays. The same organization set up a homestay for us in Toronto with a

Jewish family. My first religious festival in Canada was attending *Purim*. For a week, I was the only Muslim attending a private Jewish school.

Would you say your family was or is religious?

Yes. My family is of mixed origins—racially, ethnically, as well as sectarian—and always devout. But the *fundo-Wahhabi-Salafi* Islam, "my way is the only Islam" way, is something that is post-petrodollars. So in my family, there was never a conflict between praying and being a modern, cosmopolitan humanist. My father did *hajj* in 1964, and *salat* is a regular feature in my home. My parents made no distinction between Muslim and non-Muslim, only good people versus not so good people. They taught me that Allah was *al-Rahman* and *al-Raheem* (the Most Gracious and the Most Compassionate) and that Islam was an inclusive, accepting, and progressive religion.

How did your family's inclusive views affect your experiences growing up?

Well, one example is from our time in England. There were few non-Christian kids at my school. Most of them had letters from their families to be excused from morning assembly where, in addition to administrative matters, the Lord's Prayer and Christian hymns were recited. My parents, however, did not want me excused. They felt that an exposure to faith was important. I loved performance and had a role in every Christmas play. My teacher, Ms. Jenkins, asked me once about my parents and the fact that they did not object to me participating in Christian plays. She was so taken by my response that Jesus was a prophet and my parents had no objections that she made a point of telling them so at the next parent-teacher meeting.

Tell me about your early life in Canada.

What about it? I was a ten-year-old fey brown boy with a heavy upper-class English accent. There were few Muslims around, and homosexuality, even in Canada, was only just becoming public and ok.

Was it easy to assimilate?

I do not consider myself assimilated. I consider myself integrated. Canadian culture is largely amorphous and undefined. It is an on-going experiment. My father was educated in England; my mother had been an English teacher back in Tanzania. English is my first language, and I spoke it with a polished English accent when we came to Canada. "The West" was not a foreign concept for us coming from British-colonized Africa. My parents' understanding of Islam is not that it is "eastern" or "western," but universal.

When did you first realize you were gay?

When I started hitting puberty—or maybe that's when it started to hit me—around age twelve, I realized that I was excited by other guys. Accepting that I was gay was a longer and harder process.

Tell me about your feelings back then about being gay and Muslim.

While open and liberal in the views and practice of Islam that my parents instilled in me, coming to terms with my emerging understanding of sexuality and my attraction for other men was a challenge for me. The story of Lot troubled—even traumatized—me. I went to bed many times over many years praying I'd wake up straight. I never did. I wrestled with how a Merciful Creator would create me this way, only to condemn me. I know this to be the experience of many LGBT Muslims and of other faiths also. I thought it was wrong. I thought I was cursed. I would pray to wake up straight. I kept praying for that many nights over the years but kept waking up still gay.

Did you know other gay Muslims growing up?

Not really. There were very few queer people of colour back in the day, even fewer who were Muslim. There were one or two others, but we generally avoided each other. I think out of fear of being outed and for fear of being marginalized by other (white) queers.

You went to school to become a lawyer. Was that something expected of you or was it something you wanted to go into?

I started university when I was sixteen. I would have completed my bachelor's at age twenty in political science or anthropology. Fearing unemployment, I decided to continue my studies and applied to law school, figuring that a law degree would be a helpful stepping stone. I love science fiction. When I was younger, I had wanted to study genetics, but I found the academic program too restrictive, so I pursued the arts. When I was only about five, I decided I wanted to be an actor. Well, I guess, in some ways, being a lawyer is being a performer.

You are very much interested in the rights of others. Where do you think that comes from?

My commitment to social justice and human dignity is entrenched in my own experience of marginalization as "the other" due to my race, my religious identity, and the expression of my sexual orientation as a visibly queer man. My parents and their roles in the community instilled the importance of active commitment to social justice and human dignity in me.

Was that why you chose to go into immigration law?

I wanted karmicly clean work. And as I have been involved in human rights work and anti-oppression activism, in addition to my family's own experience with persecution and flight, it seemed appropriate. Plus, in doing the kind of refugee work that I do, there is overlap with anthropology, which is a passion.

Where does your interest in anthropology stem from?

I am fascinated by human culture and systems that perpetuate those cultures and norms. I guess, in part it is connected to my own search for identity and community. Understanding the interconnections between culture, belief, environment and class, gender, orientation, and race is interesting. Learning how they impact one another, and how they affect the structuring of human society is not only fascinating, but vital to human survival and growth in today's world.

You are known for your experience with gay refugee cases.

Yes. It is what I am known for; about 80% of my casework is representing refugees who are LGBTQ, women fleeing gender violence/persecution, and people living with HIV/AIDS.

Tell me a bit more about your refugee work.

In 1993, I opened up my own law firm doing refugee and immigration law, work I was very passionate about. My activism in the LGBT communities led to referrals of mostly gay and bisexual men seeking asylum on account of their sexual orientation. My clients have come from over a hundred different countries from Latin America, Africa, the Caribbean, Asia, and Eastern Europe. In many of these countries, same-sex activity and relationships are criminalized or "public morality" laws are used to target, marginalize, and persecute LGBT people. There were very few such claims in the mid-1990s, and a lot of unfamiliarity and even uncertainty in the law.

Asylum on the basis of sexual orientation or gender identity was a new area of refugee law when I began my practice. One of my earliest cases was that of Jose Ortigoza, a gay man from Venezuela, who filed for refugee protection when he was detained by Canadian Immigration. His claim had an extraordinary number of sittings at the Canadian Immigration and Refugee Board (IRB)– eight in total when the average is one or two. At one of the sittings, there were over twenty-three observers from human rights NGOs including Amnesty International and others, when generally there are few observers if any. Eventually, Jose was determined to be a Convention refugee and allowed to remain in Canada. The case brought awareness to a variety of immigrant/refugee advocacy groups of the particular needs and barriers facing LGBT refugees and the need for refugee organizations to address their needs. Most refugee claims are in private. Jose's hearing, upon application by the media, was public and is listed in the Canadian Library of Parliament. It led to the IRB introducing sensitivity training on LGBT human rights issues.

Is it safe to say that your legal work reinforced your activism?

Yes. My work on behalf of my clients necessarily explores the impact of the criminalization of sodomy, and of public morality laws on the lives of LGBTQ people. It also deals with how LGBTQ people are marginalized, stigmatized, and targeted in public discourse by politicians, religious leaders, and others. I also represent all women, regardless of their sexual orientation and gender identity or expression, who fear or are fleeing gender based violence. The understanding and use of international human rights concepts and decisions is integral to my representation and advocacy of queer asylum seekers. As a result, I address issues around mental and physical health as well as barriers including homophobic, racial, and religious stereotypes that negatively impact LGBTQ immigrants and refugees. In addition, I am often called to critique and assess government policies, institutions, and legislation for differential impacts especially on women and LGBTQ people.

You started Salaam back in 1991. Tell me what led to its creation.

When I moved to Toronto in 1989, I started meeting other queer Muslims who identified as Muslim and as queer. I thought, "Yes! I am not the only one!" Some had issues with being Muslim, or gay, or both. Some seemed to want to embrace both identities. So, I founded Salaam in 1991 as part of my own search for community. Queer Muslims face persecution in many Muslim countries, and even in the West we are marginalized and stigmatized by mainstream Muslim communities. Salaam was a safe space for queer Muslims at a time when we did not have many safe spaces.

What was it like being part of a group like that?

I was pleased with the initial responses and the number of responses. It was very exciting to be doing something like that, and also a little frightening. It was pre-internet and I had no idea who or what was out there.

Why did you dissolve the group?

I dissolved the group for a number of reasons. One included a death threat to a student newspaper that had published an article written by me and a couple of other Salaam members about being Muslim and gay. The threat was written by four cells of the Islamic Jihad operating out of four Ontario universities. While there were over one hundred people on the Salaam contact list, including folks in New York and even Washington State and California, the local folks were all concerned about their identities, their families' knowing, or being exposed. Communication was by phone. Everyone had their specific instructions on what to say and not to say if they were called.

It was a lot of work, and while many people liked Salaam and had great ideas, people were hesitant to take on any of the work because of their own concerns and worries. Too many people thought I had all the time, all the money, and no fear or family like they did.

So after the threat, I said, "One person does not a movement make. Maybe now is not the right time." I shut down operations in 1993.

And then you reinstated the organization in the late 1990s and it is still going on.

Faisal Alam has said that he heard about Salaam and started looking for us, but we had already closed down by then. With the advent of the internet, he put the word out—looking for other queer Muslims. Hence, the Al-Fatiha gathering in New York City in 1998. After Al-Fatiha started in New York City, a chapter was opened up in Toronto. I was only involved from afar as support for Mohammed, a young gay Muslim man who started the chapter. About two years later, we decided to go back to using Salaam as our name. We still had name recognition, so there was continuity; it was Canadian as opposed to American, and since many people thought Al-Fatiha was too religious sounding, we reclaimed the name Salaam. The group's original name was "Salaam -- a social/support group for lesbian and gay Muslims." Now we call ourselves "Salaam:

Queer Muslim Community." I suggested the word "community" because it was, and continues to be, an aspiration for the creation of a network of people with a sense of belonging—something I believe to be necessary and vital for people who are often taught to hate themselves in God's name from early childhood because of their sexual orientation, gender identity or expression. I see Salaam's work as helping to end the social schizophrenia between public and private and the self-hate so prevalent among many LGBTI Muslims as a result of rejection and demonization by their cultures and societies, generally in the name of Islam and their visions of God.

Tell me about the Salaam conference.

The conference, held in June 2003, drew more than 150 registered participants from Canada, the United States, New Zealand, England, and other places. At the gathering, on June 20, Ghazala Anwar became the first female *imam* of a public mixed-gender congregation in Canada. The participants in the prayer service included Muslims and non-Muslims, queers and straight people. Her *khutba* was about establishing *juma* services and building community. Over one hundred people participated in the prayer. My partner Guy and I prayed in the first row, a straight Iranian woman prayed between us. Though she claimed not to be a believer, she shed a tear or two during the service, as did many others in the room. The service and the deliberate choice of a female imam linked the struggles for justice on the basis of gender with the struggles for justice and dignity of LGBT people.

The issue of female imams and women's rights seems to come up repeatedly. As a gay man, why is this so important to you?

As we planned the conference, gender equality came to the forefront. I have always seen the advancement of women's equality as a struggle that parallels the one for queer human rights. I believe that homophobia and misogyny are flipsides of the same coin that is patriarchy. Many Muslim gay men don't recognize that, although they have male privilege that allows them to enter the front door of the mosque, they are loathed because they "choose" to be penetrated, and are hence like women, and ergo lesser than "real" men.

What else was special about the Salaam Conference?

A regular participant in Salaam events, David, a gay Sephardic Jewish man, had wanted to volunteer at the conference. He registered late and was told that we did not need any more volunteers. I suggested that we not turn away volunteers as some could not afford the registration fee. Less than a week before the conference, I received an email from a gay Muslim conference participant from the United Kingdom requesting an American Sign Language (ASL) translator. Allah works in mysterious ways, as David was the only person at the conference who knew ASL.

How active is Salaam in the larger queer community?

Salaam's reach and impact has been greater than one limited to queer Muslims. We are known in the community and have worked with other communities including the 519, GLAD (Gays and Lesbians of African Descent), ASAAP (Alliance for South Asian Aids Prevention), Mirchi (queer South Asian women's group), and many others including the Inside Out Film Festival, Canadian Muslim Union, Muslims for Progressive Values, APAA (Africans in Partnership Against AIDS), and others. We are working on a potential project with Egale Canada. A number of our members and board, past and present, are also active in the larger queer communities. Our profiles add to Salaam's profile.

We have also outreached to straight Muslims and particularly women, as well as non-Muslim queers. Our support group, originally facilitated by Farzana Doctor and Suhail Alsameed, has helped many people reconcile their faith and sexual orientation. Carol Chery, a young queer woman and a Jehovah's Witness, started coming to the Salaam Support Group. As a person of faith, she had difficulty in coming to terms with her faith and her orientation. It was the Salaam support group that helped her in her journey. She remains a supporter of Salaam and regularly attends our activities including the annual Salaam/Peace Iftar with her wife, Stephanie James.

How involved are you with the Salaam organization now?

I am still on the board. We are currently in the process of revitalizing the Salaam board and have several new members. While former members have stepped away from the board, they remain involved and engaged with the group.

We all have people or events in our lives that mold us into becoming who we are. Do you have such a pivotal person or moment you could share with us?

My life journey is incomplete without mention of my first partner, Guy Lahaie, and my parents.

Guy was a Franco-Ontarian and an ex-Catholic. Having been introduced to evangelical Christianity by some family members, Guy was very spiritual but weary of organized religion and any who claimed to have exclusive title to the Truth and to being 'saved'. He helped me open up my understanding of Islam. It was Guy who first began to challenge my own gendered and cultural assumptions and biases that flavored my Islam. He helped me begin to articulate and challenge my consciousness on the exclusion of women from the position of *imam*. These unarticulated doubts combined with my own ambivalence around the story of Lot were the starting point of my quest for answers that led me to create Salaam and Min-Alaq, a nascent "progressive" Muslim group I was involved in creating and which functioned from 1991 till 1994. Those are the foundation for my ongoing work since.

Five years into our relationship, Guy was diagnosed with advanced HIV infection. Guy helped me see how lucky we were; that the glass was half full, even if it was also half empty. Despite his many struggles with his health and with medication, Guy had a zest and relish for life.

In early 2003, I was asked to organize the Salaam/Al-Fatiha conference. When I asked his opinion whether I should assume the role, citing my concern for his health and our safety, he told me that if we did not do this, who would? Guy joined Salaam's board and through this also journeyed towards his embrace of Islam.

You lost Guy only months after the Salaam conference. Can you tell me about that experience?

Guy passed away at about 3:30 a.m. on February 22, 2004 at home, in my arms, with loved ones surrounding us. Later that evening I stepped out of the house for some fresh air and space. As I looked up in the sky, I saw the perfect star and crescent. It was the first day of Muharram, the first month of the Islamic calendar and the month in which Imam Hussain was martyred. I knew that Guy was at peace.

The funeral was held on Tuesday at a local church. Our friend Raven Rowanchild and I had put together an interfaith service that included recitations and readings from the Old and New Testaments, Psalms, the Qur'an and Sikh hymnals. Over three hundred people came to the funeral. United Church of Canada Minister Cheri di Novo officiated the service, at the end of which I led the *janaza*, the funeral prayer, within the sanctuary of the church. As always, everyone was invited to join and most people did.

My father and our friend Nur Marcus, a Sufi, led the *zikr* as we carried Guy's coffin out of the church to the crematorium where we continued to chant "La Illaha ill Allah" as I lit the flames. I felt blessed to have my parents and friends with me.

Guy's passing ended one chapter of my life. My healing came through the love of my family and friends and my certainty of God's love and divine plan. That did not make my days or nights easy. I made a conscious choice not to look for a new relationship soon after.

How has the experience of losing someone you loved so dearly to HIV/AIDS affected your life and work?

Prior to Guy's diagnosis in 1993, I was well aware of the human rights issues raised by the HIV/AIDS epidemic because of the loss of friends, and through clients who were HIV-positive gay asylum seekers. Through my relationship with Guy, however, I became exposed on a first-hand basis with HIV-related stigma and discrimination. I also experienced stigma and discrimination upon his death, as many imputed that I am HIV-positive, though by the grace of God, I am not. HIV/AIDS has profoundly impacted my life, and combating HIV/AIDS stigma and discrimination is an agenda that I have integrated into my professional and social justice work.

You also emphasized the influence of your parents.

I am indeed blessed by my parents, Gul and Aziz Khaki, and owe them much. My father has been a human rights/social justice activist all his life. I guess I get my zeal for community organizing, politics, and social justice from him. However, it is my mother who has been my support and my backbone, my friend, and my teacher. I owe her for her determination, inner strength, courage, and her unconditional love and support for me, even when it has not always been easy for her.

Muslim parents are not known for being accepting of their gay child. Your parents are an exception. Do you engage each other on the issue of your orientation?

While my parents never rejected me because of my sexual orientation, their acceptance of it has been a process. Their humanism challenged by their traditionalism, they knew many LGBT people but would prefer their son to be straight.

I am truly thankful for my parents and their vision of Islam that they instilled in me. I am well aware that my orientation and some of my views have been a challenge to them. I'd like to think that they too have grown in their Islam and their humanity.

Tell me about your involvement with the New Democratic Party.

Running for political office was another way for me to push the envelope.

In 2007, I was awarded the Stenert-Ferreiro Award, Canada's biggest recognition of leadership in the LGBTQ community, honouring our unsung heroes who work to achieve understanding and change. At that point, I asked Allah "What do I do next?" My city councilor and former Member of Parliament were both present at the awards ceremony. It came up that the NDP were looking for a candidate to run in the by-election. The NDP is the left-of-centre party in Canada. I have been long associated with it. I made a call: I was signed up and eventually won the nomination.

I have run for federal Member of Parliament twice as a candidate with the NDP—in the March 2008 by-election and in the October 2008 federal election. Had I been elected, I would have been the first queer Muslim to be elected to a federal parliament.

How did being Muslim and gay affect your candidacy, do you think?

Well, among other things, in trying to solicit support, I spoke to another NDP candidate who is Bengali and asked him to help me form some connection with the 5000-plus Bengalis who live in my riding (electoral area). He informed me that they had refused to support me because I was openly gay. The perverse truth is that they had no problem supporting openly gay candidates that were not Muslim. The City Councilor and Member of provincial parliament were both openly gay men who were married to their partners. Yet, despite my work and positioning on immigration, housing, homelessness and other issues, some of the Muslims in my riding rejected me because I was Muslim and gay. Pathetic is the word that comes to mind. After my second campaign, I was happy to fade out of the political limelight. At least for now.

Tell me about your current relationship.

I have been in this relationship for four years. My partner, Troy Jackson, is "black Scotian" of mixed African, Native, and European descent. He is a truly lovely human being, and I am thankful to have him in my life. By day, he manages my law firm. He is also a singer. A video for his single, "The Batty Boys Revenge," addresses the issue of homophobia and violence against queers.

Troy uses singing and song-writing as a means of social change and consciousness raising. Muslims often say that Allah loves beauty. Troy helped bring beauty into my life through his music and his heart..

Troy embraced Islam at some undefined moment after we started dating. His choice. I had simply told him at the beginning that I was Muslim and that this was important to me. I asked him to participate with me in the important events and occasions, as I was willing to do so with him for what he felt was important.

We have just come back from doing *umrah* with my parents, aunt Dolly and cousin Salim. It was an amazing experience. We have made the *niyat* to go again, *Insha'Allah*.

In 2009, Troy and I co-founded "Human+," a project dedicated to exploring the intersectionalities of our common humanity. Also in 2009, we co-founded with Dr. Laury Silvers the "el-Tawhid Juma Circle"—a queer- and woman-positive egalitarian and inclusive Muslim Friday prayer space. We have now been functioning on a weekly basis for twenty-four months. Since then, two other "el-Tawhid" communities have formed in Washington D.C. and Atlanta, Georgia. We are currently networking with people in Canada, the United States, the United Kingdom, South Africa and other places to begin similar spaces. We hope this endeavor, along with other existing inclusive prayer spaces in Los Angeles and New York City, will revolutionize many Muslim communities.

You mentioned going to umrah recently with Troy, your parents, and other close relatives. Do you care to share some of your impressions with us?

It is hard to describe. For those that know me, that's saying a lot! I was awed. Transformed. It was a spiritually and visually breathtaking experience. I think we all cried at the first sight of the Ka'aba. There were so many contrasts and paradoxes. We were painfully aware that we had to be careful and "discreet." Despite all the issues, to be in prayer with 800,000 people in close proximity was truly stunning. There were many highlights, but the ones I will cherish the most are the hours I spent at the Ka'aba in prayer and conversation with my partner and my family, and especially our last prayer in Mecca where I stood in *salat* with my mother and aunt, my father and my partner— together in the Ka'aba, something we sadly cannot do in other mosques around the world, not even in Medina.

You and Troy have done so much together. Now that gay marriage is legal in Canada, would you ever get married?

Yes. I would want to have a *nikah*. Troy and I are also about to start the process of adoption as we would like to have kids. I told Troy that he will have to decide when he is ready and ask me. I'm waiting.

So what should we expect from you next?

As part of my spiritual journey and growth, I formally joined a Rifai Sufi community last year in 2010. In addition to performing *umrah*, I also attended the al-Jama'a LGBT Retreat just outside Philadelphia. Another amazing and transformative experience. Currently, I am organizing "al-Inshirah – An Expansion of the Heart: Building for Tomorrow" Salaam Outgames Human Rights conference that will take place in Vancouver in July 2011.

This year, I have been asked to be part of the "Envisioning Global LGBT Human Rights" Project, which examines British-inherited sodomy laws and the responses by queer activists and movements. The project aims to look at India and South Africa, as well as several countries in British East Africa and the Caribbean. India and South Africa serve as points of reference where sodomy laws have been successfully overturned and where queer communities and activists face ongoing challenges in creating accepting societies. As part of this project, I recently visited Kenya, Zanzibar, Botswana, and South Africa, where the team and I met with a variety of queer and other human rights groups and organizations.

I'd like to have a television show that explores progressive and creative thought, people and issues. As I said before, I have wanted to be an actor since I was five years old. I'd love to host a show that is a critical and intersectional exploration of society and the rich tapestry that is human culture as manifested by people and groups around the globe today.

And what would you say to those inspired by your story?

There remains much work to be done to create, nurture and foster inclusive *tawhidic* Muslim spaces where diversity and inclusivity are celebrated, not just given lip service. The inherent dignity of every human being regardless of gender, gender identity, orientation, race, linguistic group, dis/ability or class must be recognized as Allah-given and exemplified by the Qur'anic declaration that Allah is closer to each one of us than our own jugular vein. While there are existing and emerging groups and communities, our challenge remains to spread the word and connect the voices into a world-transforming force. *Insha'Allah*.

Questioning the Answers

By Ahmed Morsy

Tuesday, September 11, 2001 began as just another sunny summer day. I had decided to sleep in. The stress of living and working in the city was taking a toll on me. My life had been revolving around a demanding job managing sales for a technology company while dealing, or rather, delaying dealing with marital problems that had been accumulating over the years.

The sunrays were starting to seep through the cheap plastic blinds, and I could feel their warmth on my face. As I drifted in and out of sleep, I heard the loud sound of a violent impact. Cursing under my breath, I finally gave up trying to sleep in and got out of bed. I was living in a newly developed neighborhood in Jersey City, surrounded by seemingly never-ending construction projects. My first thought was that a prefabricated wall had fallen from one of the construction cranes. While I flirted with various theories of what might have happened, my home office phone rang. My inside sales representative out of New Hampshire was on the line. "Ahmed, did you hear what happened?" she anxiously asked. "What happened?" I replied. "A missile just hit the World Trade Center. Don't you live nearby?" I ran to the window and pulled up the blinds. From my sixteenth-floor apartment looking across the Hudson River to Manhattan, I saw the North Tower, still standing high, but wounded, with an enormous gash releasing thick grey and black smoke into the clear blue sky.

I hung up the phone and frantically turned on the TV; CNN was reporting the possibility of a missile, probably an airplane as the culprit. A live picture of the twin towers was transmitted on the screen while reporters talked, some frantically, some calmly as if they still hadn't accepted the gravity of the situation. Suddenly, I saw an airplane fly behind the North Tower and disappear for a moment before I heard the sound of its impact with the South Tower, both in real time and then, a split second later, on TV.

Until today, almost ten years later, I find it quite challenging to describe the complex and even contradictory emotions I felt that day, as if my neurons were misfiring in every direction. My initial reaction was a combination of shock, disbelief, sadness, and anger, but there was also a rather strange and unexpected element of calmness and numbness, as if my own brain was tricking me to rationally face the unbearable.

I attempted to call family and friends in Manhattan, but the phone lines were jammed. I decided to go down to the street where I saw people rushing out of office buildings, while others pulled out their cameras to take photos. Some people were gathered around street vendors listening to the news as it came on the radio. An announcement was made that an American Airlines flight had just crashed into the Pentagon. All at once, it became evident that we were witnessing a highly organized attack against America.

Suddenly a complete shift in my attitude occurred as I registered people's anger in front of me while the twin towers burned behind me. "I hope these were not Muslim terrorists," I mumbled. Immersed in my thoughts and considering different "what if" scenarios, I heard screaming and a mass gasp. As I looked over my shoulder, I could see across the Hudson the South Tower collapsing in a thick cloud of smoke and debris consuming the air around it. The view seemed surreal, out of a science fiction or horror movie. Even though I was watching it collapse with my own eyes, something in me could not accept the fact that indeed it was. Less than thirty minutes later the North Tower fell, and after dominating the skyline of New York City for more than thirty years, the World Trade Center was no more. Manhattan, New York, America, the world, and I would never be the same again.

Prior to these horrific events, I had been living in the New York City area for almost ten years, having migrated from my homeland of Egypt only a few weeks after graduating from the University of Alexandria. Despondent over the trauma caused by my father's abusive treatment of me and my mother, even while she was dying from lung cancer, disgusted with the state of political affairs and lack of opportunity, I had decided to leave my homeland and the only place I knew in life. I set out to follow a path of much uncertainty and struggle in the hope that one day, I could be something, count for something, and speak my mind without fear of judgment. I could say what I wanted to say and not what I was expected to say.

The society I grew up in prides itself on strong family bonds. Parents are expected to stand by their children and support them, but my own father broke the mold, and always treated me and my mother as a burden. My mom was a beautiful woman, a college graduate who was both responsible and committed to her family. She worked longer hours than my father, rushing home afterward to prepare a hot meal for us, and took care of our home with pride and dignity. She loved me in her own way. I had no doubt she cared for me tremendously, but she was reserved in showing her emotions, and her personality was always overshadowed by my father's. I was the only child and spent countless hours in my room alone, taking comfort in studying and being a good student. And in reading. I loved to read, especially about science. Astronomy and oceanography were my favorite subjects. Perhaps I liked them because I was a dreamer, and these two subjects allowed me to go on a mental journey to a world vast and intriguing, full of possibilities and unknowns, away from my limited and sometimes harsh reality.

My extended family in Egypt was my refuge, my pride and joy. The thing I most enjoyed in my childhood was the time I spent with my aunts, uncles, and cousins. We all lived in the same upscale suburb of Alexandria, which allowed us to visit each other quite often, especially during the holy month of *Ramadan*, when we would take turns gathering in each other's apartments to break our fast. Afterward, the men would engage in political discussions, complaining about the corruption, lack of democracy and inflation, and the women would talk about social issues or swap food recipes. The kids would just be kids and play or watch some of the special *Ramadan* soap operas on TV with the rest of the family.

When I reached high school, the ever-so-touchy subject of what career path I would choose had to be discussed. Since I was a young boy, I had always wanted to be an astrophysicist or an oceanographer. My father was completely opposed to both; his rationale was that there were no career opportunities for those fields in Egypt, and that I would end up being a teacher just like him, struggling to make ends meet. Instead he proposed what I dreaded but rather expected: I should choose to study either medicine or engineering. Then he invoked a verse from the Qur'an, "It may be that you hate something when it is good for you." I knew that the reason why these were my only career choices was due to social perception: Egyptian society holds these two professions in high regard. My dream was being crushed under the weight of social expectations. I had to conform to what society deemed desirable so that my father and my family could be proud. I asked my extended family to intervene, but they sided with him. I had no choice but to concede. I chose to study architectural engineering rather than medicine only because I didn't want to go to medical school for seven years.

That incident marked the beginning of my discontent with the state of affairs of Egyptian society. I started seeing everything from a very critical and sometimes cynical perspective: A media controlled by a government that only tells people what it wants them to know. Rigged elections, corrupt politicians, police brutality; economic and political power consolidated in the hands of a select few; and rampant nepotism, where your success is mostly determined by who, rather than what you know. On the personal level, I started analyzing, and sometimes over-analyzing, how some of my friends were treated by their parents; I saw the support and compassion that my own father withheld.

I was also bothered by exclusive religious thinking. Why did some Muslims believe that you could only go to heaven if you were Muslim? There must be good Christians; I knew some of them, and they were my friends. I was sure there were nice Jews as well although I had never met a Jewish person.

Religion has always played a central role in Egyptian society. After all, religious beliefs gave us the pyramids. Egypt is the place where Judaism emerged and early Christian theology evolved. Until today, Egypt, with its one-thousand-year-old Al-Azhar University, is known as the beating heart of the Islamic world. Egyptians have always been deeply religious, whatever their faith. References to God are common in casual conversations. People usually pepper their talk with phrases such as "If God wills it," "God forbid," or "May God bless you." Religion provides the people with a sense of community in a society where poverty is rampant. Alms-giving, by those with means provides the poor with much-needed supplementary income. I remember my mother and my aunts trying to find poor people to help so that they could fulfill their religious obligations. It was religion that provided people, including myself, with a sense of belonging, a refuge for those who have been victimized by the injustices surrounding them. There were, however, people who claimed to be religious, but whose hearts were hardened, not only towards non-Muslims, but towards their fellow Muslims who did not live up to their standards and interpretations.

Reflecting on these limitations and inequalities, I decided that I must go away and find an alternative. I needed a different, more enriching experience. I needed diversity of thoughts, ideals, languages, religions, and race. I wanted to know what lies beyond the vast oceans, how other cultures think, operate, and, yes, how they perceive us. Living in Egypt inflicts many of its sons and daughters with the disease of self-deprecation, not only as individuals, but as a society. Egyptians are often torn between the memory of the greatness of their past and the sad reality of their present, and between these two extremes, they are unable to plot their exact coordinates in the human story. Sometimes we feel a sense of shame that we could not carry the torch of our ancestors, that we somehow failed them. We keep looking for a reason; society blames the government, and the government blames everything under the sun but itself, from colonialism to Zionism to religious extremism to illiteracy, and everything in between. Little did I know at the time, that people think they are only worth as much as what their government makes them believe. Instead of providing its citizens with a sense of inclusion, the Egyptian government made us feel like refugees in our own homeland. When it came to our present reality, we had nothing to be proud of, nothing to offer, maybe except for the fact that we made great falafel and kabobs.

In college, I experienced firsthand the nepotism and dysfunction of the educational system, and my disillusionment reached new heights. Many professors treated us with extreme disrespect. They overloaded us with projects that we could barely accomplish, forcing us to stay up all night, day after day to meet deadlines, only to have professors ridicule our work in the most demeaning way rather than professionally criticize it. Students with connections usually received the highest grades.

During that time, my mother was struck with cancer, and we soon learned that it was terminal. Ironically, my father's abusive behavior only increased. He started making demeaning statements about how he did not want to care for sick people, how he did not want to have sick people in his life. My father's behavior shackled me with fear; to me he was the personification of the injustice, tyranny, and constraints of the society I lived in. I spent countless nights crying in my room, wishing I had a different father. I wanted to love my dad like a son should, but how can you love someone you are terrified of, someone who is uncompromising, who refuses to communicate? I was tormented by my mother's suffering and my father's lack of sympathy. Not only did she have to endure the anguish of cancer, but also the pain of being humiliated while on her deathbed.

My aunts and I took it upon ourselves to care for my ailing mother. Two years later, and one month before my graduation, my mother lost her battle to cancer and passed away. That was in June of 1991.

My anger at my father reached a breaking point, and I decided I could not live with him anymore. In July, I was granted a US visa, and a month later, two months after my mother's passing, I landed at JFK airport.

My first reaction to New York was one of confusion; in my simple and rather ignorant mind, I was expecting to see the stereotypical image of America familiar from Hollywood movies. Instead, I encountered a city with more diversity than I had ever imagined: people of all ethnicities and religious backgrounds; more people speaking English with an accent than not; Middle Eastern street vendors selling shish kabob in Manhattan; and Hasidic Jews going about their day. And no one seemed to mind coexisting with anyone else. I realized then that getting to know the real America was going to be a long but worthwhile journey.

I spent my first few days trying to uncover the mysteries of this enormous city. I visited the Statue of Liberty and learned for the first time that Lady Liberty was originally intended to stand at the entrance of the Suez Canal in Egypt, and to look like an Egyptian peasant woman bringing the light of progress from Europe to the East. I then took off to the World Trade Center observation deck. The twin towers dominated the skyline of Manhattan, symbolizing power and progress, and the human desire to defy the odds and push technology to its limits. Later on, I decided to walk towards South Street Sea Port. Strolling down Fulton Street, I saw two Hasidic Jews walking in front of me, immersed in a conversation. I couldn't help but eavesdrop; one was apparently telling the other about his daughter's fiancé and how he thanked God that she had met someone so nice. While this incident might seem grossly insignificant to most Americans, it was the first time ever that I had experienced the human face of a Jew. It was my first realization that it was unfair to render a group of people with the same brush, and that the propaganda machine back in Egypt that was branding Jews as evil or as conspiring to control the world was simply not doing them justice. No one group of people that share the same ethnicity or religion can ever be homogeneous in their thinking.

Little did I know that only a few years later, my own people would be subjected to similar stereotyping, accused en masse of attempting to subjugate the polity of the world or install an Islamic caliphate in America, of being religious fanatics out to destroy the West. Like any other nation, we have the liberal, the moderate, the conservative. We also happen to have the Muslim equivalents of David Koresh, the Unabomber, and the Oklahoma City bomber. In fact, far from being homogenous, the so-called "Muslim world" is a mosaic of cultures, languages, and histories, and in many cases traditions that are rooted in the historical heritage of the locality, rather than stemming from the teachings of Islam.

For far too long the Arab and Muslim masses have been squeezed between the forces of authoritarianism and foreign interests. These forces left virtually no room for an average Arab or Muslim to discover, let alone express him- or herself. That sociopolitical dynamic allowed extremism to flourish. The lack of space for individuality presented enough of a playing field for Al-Qaida and others to capitalize on hopelessness and despair. If the terrorism phenomenon, as some claim, was indeed a manifestation of the desire of Islam to subjugate or declare war against the West, then why do the vast majority of terror victims also happen to be Muslim? The real war we are in is not a war between East and West, or Islam and Christendom; it is a war between the forces of ignorance and the forces of enlightenment wherever they may be, whatever culture they are from or religion they claim to follow. Humans have evolved by leaps and bounds when it comes to technological progress, but when it comes to consciousness, we are still lagging behind. To many of us, tribalism and the sense of our own superiority are the dominating ideology.

A few weeks after my arrival in New York City, it was time to roll up my sleeves and get to work. Although I had inherited a small sum of money from my mother, it wasn't enough to cover all my expenses. I needed to work. Lacking work experience that fit my level of education, I ended up taking a job in a bagel shop owned by three Israelis. Again, I was able to experience what it was like to deal with people I had never imagined associating with, people that were supposed to be my enemy. I was excited yet wary in the beginning, for I wasn't sure how I would be treated, nor how I would be perceived. Working with Israelis was my first step towards formulating and evolving my views towards humanity. The experience allowed me to put a human face on "the enemy;" I saw them laugh, we laughed together. I saw them eat, we ate together. We talked about politics, agreed and disagreed, but we were always respectful of one another. I watched my Israeli bosses discussing politics amongst themselves; the debate would get so heated sometimes that they would start yelling or gesturing with their hands, like any Middle Easterner would do. I once walked up to the manager's office, a Jew of Moroccan descent, only to find him eating feta cheese and watermelon. I had thought of that peculiar combination as an exclusively Egyptian dish. "You eat that?" I asked enthusiastically. "Of course, it's very popular in Israel," he replied. I realized then how little I knew, and how much I still needed to learn.

Later that day, I was watching TV at home when I heard one of the most empowering statements ever, "We strive for a generation that would not only answer the questions, but question the answers." Question the answers; I realized then, that that had been my mantra all along. That was what I had been longing for all my life in Egypt. There are no limits to human intelligence; theories are just that; they can be challenged. All forms of knowledge are as dynamic as the universe we live in. Human consciousness is in a constant state of evolution, and each generation contributes a little and readjusts the path a little; older conceptions can be revoked to give way to newer more relevant ones. That was the society I wanted to live in; a society that allows you to thrive, respects your individuality, and does not judge you for not conforming to the mainstream ideology. In such a society, I could be myself, choose a path that I believe in for myself, and allow my intellect to organically evolve in a direction that my soul desires, without fear of judgment or reprisal.

Despite my anger towards my father, I found myself trying to keep in touch with him. As I had done many times before, I was forcing myself to do something I did not want to do; after all I still came from a society that condemns children that are not obliging and compassionate towards their parents. He was completely unemotional towards me. He even told me that he had remarried, so if I ever came back to Egypt, I should not expect to go back home. I found myself one day bursting into tears while speaking with him. I asked him why he was treating me that way. His response was that if he was causing me emotional pain, then maybe I should not contact him anymore. I found out later that he had been lying about his marriage; that was when I decided there was no point in calling him. He died eight months later.

As I was working and getting ready for school, I was overwhelmed by a sense of loneliness and loss. I felt I had absolutely no one to turn to. A friend of mine suggested I start dating. I turned to *The Village Voice*, a free and hip local newspaper where you could place an ad with an anonymous phone extension. I went out on a few dates, but I wasn't interested in anyone. A few weeks into it, I decided it was a waste of time, and I wasn't going to renew. Ten minutes before the ad was to expire and, with it, the private mailbox, I decided to check it one last time. I took down the phone number, and a few nights later, sitting alone on my couch, I decided to call.

A soft voice answered the phone and asked me for my name. I said "Mike," the American name one of the owners of the bagel shop had bestowed upon me. Of course, I could not hide my accent, so she asked me where I was from. I said "Egypt," and she responded in broken Arabic, "*Ana yahudia amrekania,*" meaning "I'm Jewish American." As it turned out, she had been to Egypt and learned a few words, curse words mostly. We went out on a first date and both felt a sense of connection. After dating for three short months, we moved in together. Of course, this was a big secret that I had to hide from my family; it would have been scandalous for them to learn that I was living with a girl. Only, after we decided to get married, and one month before the wedding, did I reveal the news to my family. As I had expected, they did not try to sway me from marrying a Jewish girl, and only asked me if she was nice and came from a nice family.

My aunts and uncles had told me on multiple occasions that they had had many Jewish neighbors when they were children back in the 1940s, many of whom were their playmates. Sometimes their parents would exchange babysitting favors. They could still remember their names, and the members of each family. Up until the mid-twentieth century, Egypt had a vibrant Jewish minority that was eighty thousand strong. The Mizrahi Jews were not considered foreign; they were an integral part of the dynamic and liberal fabric of the society at the time. They either had or had adopted Arabic names that were indistinguishable from the names of their Muslim neighbors. Jewish movie stars like Laila Mourad, and Raqya Ibrahim were national sensations. Top composers such as Dawood Hosni made enormous contributions to Egyptian music and composed for the legendary singer Umm Kulthum. It was not until the creation of the State of Israel and especially after the Lavon scandal that things took an ugly turn between the Jews of Egypt and the regime of former president Gamal Abdel Nasser. I believe this is why you don't find this hatred of anything Jewish among that older generation, for they knew the human Jew, not the surreal image conjured up in the imagination of my generation by the poisonous rhetoric projected by the mass media and religious extremists.

I also got to know my fiancée's parents and their spouses. Initially, I wasn't sure how they would feel about me, or where they stood on the ideological scale regarding their daughter marrying an Arab man. After a few dinners with them, we warmed to one another and I felt more comfortable with them, so much so that they reminded me of my own family in some regards. Politically liberal, socially conservative, I certainly felt I was in my comfort zone. Over time I got the chance to meet their neighbors, friends and extended family. No one seemed to be opposed to the idea of having an Arab man in their lives, far from it. The only exception was my wife's grandmother's seventy-seven-year-old boyfriend; I never got to meet him, but I was told he was adamantly opposed to my becoming part of the family. He was an Austrian Jew and a Holocaust survivor, and I understood that he had lost many members of his family and was scared because of his experience. I assume his view of the world revolved around his painful past, something I can personally relate to, even though I have always resisted falling captive to my own. My wife's grandmother's relationship with him was strained over me, and I had to tell her to let it be, and not to try to challenge his position towards me.

My journey continued with the start of the school year; I would work at the bagel shop from nine till five, and then rush to school to attend evening classes from six till ten. By the time I got home it was already eleven, which left me very little time to work on my assignments. I would spend all day Saturday at the lab working on computer animation projects. Six months later I was recommended by a professor for a teaching assistance position twice a week assisting undergraduate students with Computer Aided Design assignments in the lab. I had to cut back on my hours at the bagel shop to keep up with my obligations at school. A few weeks later, I was approached by another professor to do some consulting work for him for about ten hours per week. My desire for more led me to bite off more than I could chew; I barely had time to enjoy life and was always stressed out. I had to make a choice between my ambition and my mental and physical well-being.

Not too long afterwards I had my first break. My school was hosting a career fair, and although I was scheduled to work at the bagel shop that day, I made a spur of the moment decision to attend the fair instead. At the career fair I was hired by a technology company as a Computer Aided Design Engineer. Consequently, I resigned from the bagel store and the consulting job.

Before I started my new job, my wife and I decided to take a few weeks off and travel to Egypt, where my wife would meet my family for the first time. They had seen pictures of us and our wedding in the past, but had not met her in person. Having been to Egypt before, my wife fit right in and didn't experience the culture shock some do; she hit it off with everyone right away. She got into the habit of showing off the few Arabic sentences she knew--of course her vocabulary of curse words had expanded by leaps and bounds since we met--but I begged her not to show off her Arabic cursing skills in front of my family.

My wife never had very good social skills. She always seemed to say the wrong thing at the wrong time in the wrong place, something that made me nervous and occasionally caused me a great deal of embarrassment. She had a very good heart and she meant well, but she had trouble controlling her anger, which was something I had experienced before with my father and which brought back painful memories

I continued working and going to school, and things began to get a little better. I wasn't as exhausted as I used to feel since I no longer had to do manual labor in the morning. I focused my energy on getting good grades and proving myself at work. It was exceptionally heartening to feel respected and encouraged by my professors at school, something I had never experienced before. My Egyptian-born architectural design professor was especially respectful and encouraging, which made me wonder why we had to endure such rogue treatment from the teaching staff back in Egypt.

For the most part, I never felt out of place at work; I can only recall one incident that made me feel very uncomfortable. I was engaged in a hallway conversation with a sales manager and a secretary, and she asked him why he lived in Brooklyn. His answer was that he lived in a Middle Eastern neighborhood because terrorists would never bomb their own people. I knew he was joking, but as they say, there's a grain of truth in every joke. So I told him with a smile that I couldn't believe he had said that, and, for his information, terrorists do bomb their own people. I understood at the time that people were still shaken by the World Trade Center bombing of 1993, but I hoped I wouldn't have to listen to such embarrassing comments again. Ironically, after that incident we started teaming up on sales calls frequently and we became good friends.

After three years on the job, working as a field engineer, I had my next big break. A former colleague had referred me to the sales director of a smaller tech company. After a few interviews, I was offered a position as sales manager, something I had been aspiring to for some time. Landing the job was something of a long-shot since sales was an area dominated by white, native-born Americans.

I started my new job with much anxiety. I wanted so desperately to prove that an immigrant could do as well as someone born and raised in America. I worked very hard, making sales calls in the morning, and followed up on them in the evening. I managed proposals, conference calls, and cold calls, which I dreaded the most. To everyone's surprise, and especially mine, I was ranked the second sales manager worldwide based on my first-year numbers. However, one can only try so hard. The dotcom bubble burst, and, with the Y2K fizzle, the impact was enormous. As it became increasingly harder to close on business, my anxiety became unmanageable, and I had trouble sleeping. I had bouts of insomnia that lasted for days. Somehow I still managed to meet my numbers the second year, but my pipeline was drying out, and I had to make more and more cold calls.

I reconsidered my priorities. A few years before, I had been like a child exploring the world for the first time, wanting to experience a bit of everything. But now, I had to ask myself whether being a sales manager was making me happy? Was making more money making me happy? Was I happy in my marriage? What did I really want out of life? There were many questions, but no particular answers presented themselves. That was my state of heart and mind on September 11.

The tragic events of that day made many New Yorkers, including me, reconsider our priorities. Life can't just be about career, net worth, market portfolios and retirement investments. There must be something more. What about enjoying the sunshine? Or having a cup of tea and a conversation with someone you love? Or, most of all, feeling content with where you are and where you are going, feeling that you are contributing to the good of humanity rather than to the growth of the value of your portfolio.

A few months after September 11, going through some old papers, I came across some notes I had taken during a meeting at Cantor Fitzgerald, the company that occupied two floors in the World Trade Center where one of the planes hit. Everyone perished except for the owner. I stopped for a minute and tried to recall all the people I had laid eyes on when I was at their offices; every single soul had perished. The symbols of power that I had been marveling at a few short years ago had collapsed, and with them every hope, emotion, and expectation of three thousand lives. No matter how hard we try to immerse ourselves in our ambitions and our hopes, the slightest breeze can extinguish the flame of life. That's how vulnerable they were, and that's how vulnerable I was, too. I could have been one of them. Life is short, and I needed to do what made me happy now, not the following year, and not the following month. That was when I decided to make radical changes to my life.

I knew I didn't want to feel anxious anymore. I wanted to be able to enjoy the small things in life one day, one hour, one minute at a time. I also knew I wasn't happy in my marriage, and I had to make the radical move of ending it.

My wife and I could no longer see eye to eye; the lack of communication was putting an enormous strain on our relationship. I could not stand her fits of anger and her unwillingness to compromise, and she could not stand what she described as my aloofness. Although our marriage did not succeed, I can admit that it was an enriching experience, an invaluable phase that was integral in shaping my understanding of the world, and most importantly, of myself.

In the process of getting to know an extended family of a different culture and different religion from my own, I got to know a family that was very familiar to me, more familiar than I would have imagined had I not left Egypt. In my wife, I did not see a Jewish woman, but a person who was trustworthy, complex, and insecure.

Within two years, I resigned from my job as sales manager and decided to do what I enjoyed more, engineering. Having always loved nature and sunshine, I moved to Southern California, where I found more personally fulfilling employment in the aerospace industry. What I look forward to now is a way to be able to contribute to humanity.

My personal journey is an American story. It is a journey of self-discovery that helped me break the shackles of fear and enabled me to understand who I am. So, what have I learned? What defines me as a person is not only being Muslim, being Egyptian, or being Arab, not even some combination of all three. I am more than the sum of my parts. What defines me is being me, a collection of diverse and sometimes contradicting, even conflicting energies. I am made up of a unique human recipe of individual consciousness that stems not only from the collective consciousness of heritage, tradition and religion, but also from an entirely unique and personal set of experiences, experiences that only I lived through and that I perceived in ways like no other person could have. These experiences managed to leave a sequence of impacts on my consciousness that are impossible to replicate or even single out. Added to this blend of experiences and impressions, is a selection of personal secret ingredients that make me even more unique. Each of us is constituted of these unique ingredients, so secret, that we may spend the rest of our lives trying to unlock the mystery of us. In this uniqueness, we are all alike.

My story is not an Islamic story, it is not an Arab story; it is a human story about one person who sought freedom and a chance for happiness. My story bears witness to the fact that our only true differences, be they ethnicity or religion, are those we have not chosen for ourselves.

Acknowledgments

The creation of this anthology has been a labor of charity and love from the progressive Muslim community. This anthology provided everyone who worked on it a space to project our voices as progressive Muslims, unshackle religious interpretation from its orthodox stronghold, create inclusive communities, and work towards a more just society.

Authors donated their work and time in exchange for only a byline. To the authors, thank you for sharing your deepest and most personal stories and for working for months with the editorial team on honing your works. Because of your bravery in sharing your personal stories, a kind of sacred text, you provide us all with the wellspring to discover our common humanity.

Less visible than the authors, but equally deserving of recognition, are the editors of this volume. The only payment editors received for their collective hundreds of hours of work was to help writers, many of whom had never published before, tell their stories in as compelling and honest a way as possible. As editors, we were privileged to be entrusted with the personal stories of our community and to play a role in amplifying their authentic voices.

Without Sara Farooqi, half of what MPV undertakes would not come to fruition. After launching the call for submissions, she continued her service to this project on the editorial team. To Zahra Ayubi and Tynan Power, your help with the editing process, your advice on style guides and in putting together the glossary helped make this project a success.

We are grateful to Reza Aslan and Aasif Mandvi for believing in the importance of this project. To Pamela Taylor, Katrina Daly Thompson, and Patricia Locke, thank you for your assistance to the editorial team.

This project was a community effort and a testament to what we can accomplish when we work together.

Vanessa Karam, R. Olivia Samad, and Ani Zonneveld

Contributors

Editors

Zahra Ayubi is a Ph.D. candidate in the Department of Religious Studies at the University of North Carolina at Chapel Hill, where she has been studying and teaching since 2007. Her areas of research are Islam and gender, classical and modern Islamic ethics, and Islam in American religious history. She earned an M.A. in religious studies at UNC Chapel Hill and a B.A. with highest honors in Islamic and Middle Eastern studies and women's studies at Brandeis University. Currently, she is an editor at *Azizah Magazine*, a quarterly American Muslim women's publication, and works with MPV.

Sara A. Farooqi is vice-chair of MPV and serves as an editor for the Literary Zikr project. She holds a bachelor's degree in sociology and Islamic cultural studies from Pitzer College. Sara is active in national advocacy efforts for LGBT/queer rights, women's empowerment and environmental justice. She is currently working on a book of poetry.

Vanessa Karam, co-chief editor, is a founding member of MPV and has served on its board of directors and advisory council. She holds a master's degree in Islamic philology, Islamic studies, and Turkic linguistics. Currently, she is working toward a doctorate in comparative religion at University of the West, a private Buddhist-affiliated university near Los Angeles, where she runs the general education program and teaches language and religion courses. Vanessa is a German-English translator and has been a professional editor for over twenty-five years. She is a passionate interfaith activist and spokesperson for socially relevant and inclusive interpretations of Islam.

Tynan Power is a transgender Muslim writer, editor, educator and activist. A progressive Muslim and interfaith leader, he was one of the original members of Al Fatiha, an LGBTQ Muslim organization founded in 1999. He is the founder of the lay-led, LGBTQ-inclusive Pioneer Valley Progressive Muslims-Jamiat al-Inshirah. Ty has spoken about Islam at numerous conferences and universities, and has taught a variety of classes designed to introduce and demystify Islam for children and adults. Ty has had the privilege of being the primary author of adaptations in MPV's Literary Zikr project. Ty lives in Massachusetts with his partner and two sons. He is also a contributing author in this anthology.

R. Olivia Samad, co-chief editor, is progressive on social issues and conservative on matters of writing and editing. She writes a bimonthly column for the *Stanford Magazine*, which she has done since graduating from Stanford with bachelor's degrees in economics and public policy. Later, as a dean's scholar at Georgetown Law focused on conflict resolution, she worked on a Human Rights Watch publication on personal status laws of Muslim women in the European Union. Olivia is an attorney who works on energy-related matters, but started as an intellectual property and commercial litigator. She worked for the District Attorney's office during the OJ Simpson trial, has prosecuted an off-duty police officer in a criminal case, handled twelve adoption hearings in one day, and won asylum for a pro-democracy Congolese activist. She chairs the board of the Asian Pacific American Dispute Resolution Center, an organization that is creating a more peaceful multiethnic city by teaching peace-building, peer mediation, and conflict resolution skills in our schools and communities. She is also a contributing author in this anthology.

Ani Zonneveld, co-chief editor, is a songwriter, producer, and activist. As a songwriter/producer she has won many awards including the 1999 and 2004 Album of the Year award at the AIMM, the Malaysian equivalent of the Grammy, and a Grammy certification for her song contribution to Keb' Mo's album *Keep It Simple*. Post 9-11 she wrote and produced the first Islamic pop album by a female singer, titled *Ummah Wake Up*, followed by *One*, an interfaith album. Uniquely blending her two worlds of music and social activism into one, Ani speaks and sings her message of social justice, human rights, and peace, from a Muslim's perspective. In 2006, she was named a Muslim Leader of

Tomorrow by the American Society for Muslim Advancement. As co-founder and Chair of MPV, she has organized interfaith arts and music festivals and participated in interfaith dialogues. Ani performs wedding services for mixed faith and gay couples.

Authors

Daayiee Abdullah is a linguist, scholar of Far East and Middle East studies, former public interest lawyer, and a specialist in shari'ah sciences and Qur'anic interpretation. He lectures on progressive Muslim concepts, interfaith networking, and inclusive revisions of Islamic theological thought and interpretations of shari'ah. He is Imam and Education Director of The Light of Reformation Mosque in Washington, D.C.; co-chapter leader of MPV-DC, and former board member of Al-Fatiha Foundation.

Ismail Butera is an accordionist residing in New York. He performs for the aged and infirm in nursing homes and hospitals, and provides music therapy for patients with the onset of dementia. His interest in the folk, spiritual, and oral traditions of the Balkans and the Near East has prompted him to share with audiences the ancient bardic stories and music of those regions, accompanying himself on a number of long-necked traditional lutes from his collection. A student of comparative religion, he feels it is important in our time to break down the dogmatist barriers between peoples and faiths and together strive for the universality that is our common goal.

Patricia Dunn was managing editor of *Muslim Wakeup!*, America's most popular Muslim online magazine with over 200,000 monthly readers, from 2003–2008. Her fiction has appeared in *Global City Review*, *Salon.com*, *Women's eNews*, *The Christian Science Monitor*, *The Village Voice*, *The Nation*, and *L.A. Weekly*, among other publications. Her work is anthologized in *Stories of Illness and Healing: Women Write Their Bodies*, Kent State University Press. Her forthcoming novel will be published by Westside Books, fall 2011. She has an MFA from Sarah Lawrence College.

Mona Eltahawy is an award-winning columnist and an international public speaker on Arab and Muslim issues. She is based in New York. Born in Port Said, Egypt in 1967, Mona has lived in the United Kingdom, Saudi Arabia, and Israel. In 2005, she was named a Muslim Leader of Tomorrow by the American Society for Muslim Advancement. She is a member of the Communications Advisory Group for Musawah, the global movement for equality and justice in the Muslim family. In April 2011 Mona was ranked number 51 among the top 100 Most Powerful Arab Women and number 124 on the 500 Arab Power List by *Arabian Business Magazine*.

Jack Fertig is a professional astrologer living in San Francisco with Elias Trevino, his partner since 1994. He was born into a family of activists and was folding and stuffing envelopes for the Congress of Racial Equality at age four. He's been in various struggles for peace, freedom, and justice. An agnostic upbringing allowed Jack to find his own spiritual path relatively free of childhood baggage. He made *shahadah* in 2003 and is now working on the novel, *Vampires in Oz*.

Yarehk Hernandez is an educator, poet, and progressive Muslim activist. He completed his undergraduate studies at the City University of New York, where he majored in Middle East history and minored in comparative religion. He completed his graduate studies at the University of Pennsylvania where he received a Master of Science in education and majored in secondary social studies/citizenship education. Yarehk has also spent time traveling and studying Ilm al-Tassawuf (Sufism). He is currently a doctoral candidate in religion at Temple University.

Nakia Jackson makes things. Sometimes it's fudge; other times, it's history. A musician, writer and rabble-rouser, her urge to create inspired her to lead the *Eid* prayer she wanted to see. Nakia attended the Berklee College of Music, and uses her finely honed musical skills to compose tunes for her son. She enjoys knitting, sewing, and other pursuits that would not be expected of a staunch feminist. She writes about Islam, music and crafts for several online publications, including *Sadie Magazine*, *Naseeb* and *Muslim Wake Up!*.

Afdhere Jama was born in Somalia, and moved to the United States as a teenager. He is the author of *Illegal Citizens: Queer Lives in the Muslim World* and *At Noonday with the Gods of Somalia*. He was the editor of *Huriyah*, a magazine published between 2000 and 2010, which was for and by the queer Muslim community. He lives in California.

El-Farouk Khaki is a refugee and immigration lawyer. His practice primarily involves representing women fleeing gender violence, LGBTQI people fleeing persecution because of their sexual orientation and/or gender identity, as well as people fleeing persecution because of their HIV status. Repeatedly, El-Farouk has been recognized for his legal work and social justice activism. The numerous awards he has received include: the 2006 Pride Toronto Excellence in Spirituality Award; the 2006 Steinert & Ferreiro Award; the 2007 Canadian Bar Association, Sexual Orientation and Gender Identity Conference Hero Award. In 2009, El-Farouk was elected Grand Marshall for the Toronto Pride Parade and was the recipient of the 'Can't Stop, Won't Stop' theme award. His float entry in the Pride Parade was titled Human+ and won the 'Best Embodiment of the LGBTTIQQ2S' Award.

Shahla Khan Salter is a lawyer by profession and mother of three, living in Ottawa, Canada. She chairs MPV Canada.

Ameena Meer is a creative director and writer. Her recent work includes fragrances and make-up for Calvin Klein and the branding and social media for park51, the Lower Manhattan Islamic Community Center. Her ad agency/gallery space in Tribeca, Take-Out Media, fuses the magic of prestige advertising with environmental and humanitarian concerns. She also blogs about her battle with cancer, single motherhood, dating, debt, and divorce court at www.ameenameer.blogspot.com. Her novel, *Bombay Talkie*, was published in 1993.

Ahmed Morsy is a senior consulting engineer at NASA's Jet Propulsion Laboratory. He holds a bachelor of science in architecture degree from the University of Alexandria, Egypt, and a master's degree in communication arts from The New York Institute of Technology. He is an advocate of human rights and intercultural dialogue.

M. Ameerah Saleem, a Washington, D.C. native, earned her bachelor's degree in psychology from Spelman College, and then managed clinical data for research protocols such as HIV/AIDS, atherosclerosis, substance dependency and abuse, and breast and cervical cancers. She has a certificate in health counseling from the Institute for Integrative Nutrition in New York, where she studied holistic philosophies and treatments. Ameerah is pursing a master's degree in community psychology at Antioch University, focusing on youth empowerment, and community health and prevention. In her spare time, she enjoys reading, volunteering, and participating in run/walks for health promotion campaigns.

Dizery Salim was born in Tokyo and grew up in Tripoli, Kuala Lumpur, Los Angeles, and London. She splits her time between Geneva, Switzerland, where she works, and New York, home to her husband. She is working on her first novel, an amusing and light-hearted look at growing up Muslim.

Sahira Traband lives in Los Angeles, California with her husband and two sons. This is her first attempt at publishing her writing.

Fact Sheet – Muslims for Progressive Values (MPV)

All proceeds from the sale of this anthology will go to MPV.

Mission Statement:

MPV is an inclusive community rooted in the traditional Qur'anic ideals of human dignity and social justice. We welcome all who are interested in discussing, promoting, and working for the implementation of progressive values—human rights, freedom of expression, and separation of church and state—as well as inclusive and tolerant understandings of Islam. Learn more about what MPV does online at http://www.www.mpvusa.org.

What we do:

MPV establishes and nurtures vibrant progressive Muslim communities. We do this by creating opportunities for religious discourse, volunteer and community activities, and cultural events bringing together the arts, spirituality and social activism.

MPV is a progressive Muslim voice on contemporary issues. We voice our perspectives by participating in civil discourse, engaging with the media and government entities, and by partnering with both Muslim and non-Muslim progressive organizations.

MPV promotes theologically-sound frameworks for Islamic liberalism. We seek to reinvigorate the Islamic tradition of *ijtihad* (critical engagement and interpretation of sacred texts) and intellectual discourse. We do this by collaborating with religious scholars and developing position papers on theological issues that are accessible to a wide audience.

Through its Literary Zikr project, MPV brings the writings of scholars of progressive Islamic thought to Muslim youth in search of answers to questions of faith, human rights, contemporary social issues, and political governance. Literary Zikr is a project that provides central ideas in the academic works of world-renowned and respected scholars of Islam in simple and youth-friendly language.

What We Stand For:

The MPV Logo features a tree with ten branches. Each branch of the tree represents one of MPV's ten principles, which are rooted in Islam.

1. **Identity**: We accept as Muslim anyone who identifies as such. The veracity and integrity of that claim is between the individual and God, and is not a matter for the state nor an issue which other individuals can or should judge.
2. **Equality**: We affirm the equal worth of all human beings, regardless of race, sex, gender, ethnicity, nationality, creed, sexual orientation, or ability. We are committed to work toward societies that ensure social, political, educational, and economic opportunities for all.
3. **Separation of Religious and State Authorities**: We believe that freedom of conscience is not only essential to all human societies but integral to the Qur'anic view of humanity. We believe that secular government is the only way to achieve the Islamic ideal of freedom from compulsion in matters of faith.
4. **Freedom of Speech**: We support freedom of expression and freedom of dissent, whether political, artistic, social or religious, even when that expression may be offensive and that dissent may be considered

blasphemous. No one should be legally prosecuted, imprisoned or detained for declaring or promoting unpopular opinions.
5. **Universal Human Rights**: We affirm our commitment to social, economic and environmental justice. We believe that the full self-realization of all people, in a safe and sustainable world, is a prerequisite for freedom, civility, and peace. We support efforts for universal health care, universal public education, the protection of our environment, and the eradication of poverty.
6. **Women's Rights**: We support women's agency and self-determination in every aspect of their lives. We believe in women's full participation in society at every level. We affirm our commitment to reproductive justice and empowering women to make healthy decisions regarding their bodies, sexuality and reproduction.
7. **LGBTQ Rights**: We endorse the human and civil rights of lesbian, gay, bisexual, transgender, intersex, and queer (LGBTIQ) individuals. We support full equality and inclusion of all individuals, regardless of sexual orientation or gender identity, in society and in the Muslim community. We affirm our commitment to ending discrimination based on sexual orientation and gender identity.
8. **Critical Analysis and Interpretation**: We call for critical engagement with Islamic scripture, traditional jurisprudence, and current Muslim discourses. We believe that critical thinking is essential to spiritual development. We promote interpretations that reflect basic Qur'anic principles of tolerance, inclusiveness, mercy, compassion, and fairness.
9. **Compassion**: We affirm that justice and compassion should be the guiding principles for all aspects of human conduct. We repudiate militarism and violence, whether on an individual, organizational, or national level.
10. **Diversity:** We embrace religious pluralism and the diversity of inspirations that motivate people to embrace social justice. We believe that one's religion is not the exclusive source of truth. As such, we will engage with a diversity of philosophical and spiritual traditions in pursuit of a more just, peaceful and sustainable world.

Glossary

adab	Arabic word for "behavior." *Adab* refers to a comprehensive Islamic code of ethics, etiquette and conduct.
adhan/azaan	Arabic word for the call to prayer, which is recited in Arabic before the five prescribed daily prayers.
Al-Fatiha	Arabic word for "The Opening." *Al-Fatiha* is the title of the first chapter of the Qur'an, a passage central to the religious life of Muslims.
alif	First letter of the Arabic alphabet.
Allah	Arabic word for "God."
Amreekah	South Asian pronunciation for "America."
angels of the tomb	Two angels who test the deceased regarding their faith after death, according to Islamic belief.
Auntie, Aunty	Term of respect for older women in the Indian subcontinent.
ayat	Arabic word for "verse" of the Qur'an.
ba	Second letter of the Arabic alphabet.
Bajram	Word used for *Eid* in Albanian and other languages of the Balkans. It is derived from the Turkish word *bayram*.
baju kurung	Malay women's traditional attire.
bhabhi	Urdu term and title for the wife of one's brother or male relative.
bid'a	Arabic word meaning "innovation." It refers to introducing practices into the religion that are not condoned by the Qur'an or *sunnah*. *Bid'a* is considered a sin.

Bismillah/ar-rahman ar-rahim	Arabic phrase meaning "In the name of God, the most Gracious the most Merciful." This phrase is frequently uttered to mark introductions or beginnings of events, such as praying, eating, drinking, setting out on a journey, etc. It is often shortened to *Bismillah*.
burkah	Loose outer garment worn by some Muslim women. It is usually black or blue in color and covers the body from head to toe, with an attached veil covering the face.
chador	Traditional body-length outerwear worn by some women in Iran. It consists of a semi-circular piece of fabric draped over the head and held closed in the front.
chapatti	South Asian flat bread.
Dar-al-Islam	Arabic phrase meaning "house/abode of Islam." It is used to refer to places where Muslims can practice their religion freely and securely. It is often used to mean countries where the majority of the population is Muslim regardless of the actual freedom of religion Muslims may enjoy there.
dawa	Arabic word meaning "issuing an invitation." It denotes preaching and inviting people to Islam in order to strengthen the community and win converts.
deen	Arabic word meaning "faith," "religion," "way of life," or "belief system."
dhikr/zhikr/zikr	Arabic word meaning "remembrance." It refers to the specific Islamic practice of remembrance of God, usually a devotional act involving the recitation of the names of God, Qur'anic verses and supplications.
doa/dua	Supplication or personal prayers uttered at any time, following or independent of ritual prayer, or *salat*.
Eid	Arabic word for "festival" or "feast," used to designate holidays in the Islamic calendar.

	Most Muslims observe two major *Eid* holidays, but some observe other minor *Eid* holidays throughout the year.
Eid al-Adha	Arabic phrase meaning "feast of the sacrifice." *Eid al-Adha* is the second of the two major holidays in the Islamic calendar. Often lasting three to five days, *Eid al-Adha* is celebrated during the Islamic month of *Dhul Hijjah* to mark the end of the *hajj* (pilgrimage to Mecca). Traditionally, sheep and other livestock are slaughtered to commemorate Abraham's willingness to sacrifice his son Isma'il (Ishmael), son of Hagar. A portion of the meat must be distributed to the poor.
Eid al-Fitr	Arabic phrase meaning "feast of the breaking of the fast." *Eid al-Fitr* is observed at the end of the fasting month of *Ramadan* and is often a three-day celebration. It is the first of the two major holidays in the Islamic calendar.
fajr	Arabic word meaning "dawn." The *fajr* prayer is the first of the five daily ritual prayers and marks the beginning of the fast each day during *Ramadan*.
Feast of the Sacrifice	See *Eid al-Adha*.
fiqh	Arabic term referring to Islamic jurisprudence.
fitna	Arabic term referring to social chaos and upheaval, especially resulting from disagreement and divisions within Islam.
FTM	Pronounced "F to M." Abbreviation for "female-to-male" transsexual or transman.
fundo	Slang for "fundamentalist."
Hadith	Recorded saying or quotation attributed to Prophet Muhammad or to his trusted companions regarding the Prophet's actions, habits, and practices. In traditional Islamic scholarship, *hadith* are the second source of Islamic law after the Qur'an.

Haji	Arabic word for someone who has performed the pilgrimage to Mecca (*hajj*). It is often used as an honorific form of address.
Hajj	Pilgrimage to Mecca instituted by Prophet Muhammad, performed during the Islamic month of *Dhul Hijjah*. *Hajj* is known as the fifth pillar of Islam, a religious duty that every able-bodied and financially capable Muslim must perform once in his or her lifetime.
halal	Arabic word for "permissible." *Halal* refers to things or acts believed to be religiously permissible or legal for Muslims.
haram	Arabic word usually translated as "forbidden" or "sinful." *Haram* refers to things or acts believed to be prohibited by Islamic law. The English word harem is derived from this word.
henna night	Pre-wedding event in many Muslim cultures, at which the bride's hands (and often feet) are intricately decorated with henna. The celebration may also include the exchange of wedding gifts, music, singing and dancing.
hijab	Arabic word for "covering," used to refer to the various types of headscarves worn by some Muslim women.
hijra	Hindi and Urdu word for transgender people assigned male at birth (similar to transwomen) and who often live in long-standing transgender communities in South Asia.
iftaar	Arabic word meaning "breaking the fast." *Iftar* is the meal eaten after sunset to break the day's fast, especially during Ramadan.
imam	Person, almost invariably male, who leads Muslims in prayer and often provides religious guidance.
Imam Hussain	The grandson of Prophet Muhammad. In Shia Islam, Hussain is revered as the third rightful successor to Prophet Muhammad after Ali, Hussain's father and Hassan, Hussain's

	brother. Hussain was killed at the Battle of Karbala, an incident the Shia regard as an act of martyrdom and commemorate every year on *Ashura*, the tenth day of the month of Muharram. The title *Imam* refers in Shia Islam to the religious, spiritual, and political leader of the *ummah*, who possesses divine knowledge and authority. Sunni Muslims also hold Hussain in high regard as a member of the Prophet's family and the last of the four "rightly guided" caliphs (*ar-Rashidun*).
Insha'Allah	Arabic phrase meaning "If God wills." It is used frequently by Muslims when making plans or stating wishes for the future. The phrase indicates that humans do not control their destiny and is used as a sign of humility and faith.
Intifada	Arabic word for "shaking off," but frequently translated as "uprising" or "resistance." In this book, it refers to the Palestinian uprising, starting in the 1980s, against Israeli occupation of the West Bank and Gaza.
Issa	Arabic name for Jesus. Muslims revere Jesus as one of the prophets who received revelation.
janaza	Islamic funeral prayer. A religious obligation, it is performed in congregation and seeks forgiveness for the deceased and all deceased Muslims.
jihad	Arabic word for "struggle" or "striving." It is often used in the Arabic expression *al-jihad fi sabil Illah*, which means "striving in the path of God" and refers to any action that is done with difficulty for the sake of God. Muslims often distinguish the greater *jihad*, the inner struggle to become a better person, and the lesser *jihad*, the outer struggle or effort engaging others. *Jihad* is often translated incorrectly as "holy war." Armed struggle is only one subcategory of *jihad* and must fulfill specific conditions and adhere to certain rules of engagement to be valid.

jihad al-nafsi	Arabic phrase meaning "struggle of the self." It refers to a spiritual struggle, the struggle against the ego.
juma/jum'ah/jumaah	Muslim weekly congregational prayer observed on Friday.
Ka'aba	Arabic word meaning "cube." The Ka'aba is a cube-shaped granite structure covered in a gold-embroidered black silk cloth. It is located in Mecca and is the holiest site in Islam. According to the Qur'an, the Ka'aba was originally built by Abraham (Ibrahim) and his son Ishmael (Isma'il). During the rituals of the *hajj* and *umrah*, pilgrims circumambulate the Ka'aba seven times. All Muslims face the Ka'aba when performing ritual prayer (*salat*).
khalifah	Arabic word meaning "vicegerent," "representative," or "successor." It refers to the theological concept of responsibility for the world installed in humankind by God. Historically, the term also has been used to describe the religio-political office of leaders who claimed to politically succeed Prophet Muhammad.
khutbah	Arabic word referring to a sermon or speech delivered in the mosque before Friday congregational prayers.
La illaha ill Allah wa Muhammad rasul Allah	Arabic phrase meaning "[I testify that] there is no god but God and [I testify] that Muhammad is the messenger of God." See also *shahada*.
LGBTQ	Abbreviation for "lesbian, gay, bisexual, transgender, and queer."
Lot	Arabic Lut. According to the Qur'an, Lot was the nephew of Abraham and a prophet. His story, associated with the cities of Sodom and Gomorrah, is similar though not identical to the Biblical account. God destroyed the twin cities because their inhabitants had turned away from Him. Their greed had led them to such inhospitality that they humiliated,

abused and raped strangers. Traditional Islamic interpretation has seen in this story of same-sex rape a condemnation of homosexuality in general, while alternate readings point to the act of rape as the unforgiveable sin.

madrassa	Arabic word for "school." It is commonly used as a name for traditional Islamic schools for religious education.
mashallah	Arabic phrase meaning "Whatever God wills." It is used by Muslims to express joy or gratitude when responding to someone's good fortune or when praising or complimenting someone. In popular belief, saying *mashallah* is held to protect the fortunate person from the envy, or evil eye, of others.
mashaykh	Plural of the word *shaykh*, used to describe Sufi masters of a specific order. It can be used to describe a group of masters.
masjid	Arabic word for "mosque." It is a place where individual and congregational prayer is performed. It can include social meeting spaces or schools. Traditionally, men and women pray in separate sections of a mosque.
mim	Arabic letter, equivalent to the English letter "m."
muezzin	Arabic word for the person who makes the Islamic call to prayer. See also *adhan*.
Mujahideen	Arabic word meaning "people who perform *jihad* (struggle)." It is often used self-referentially by groups that wage armed struggles of resistance or rebellion in order to suggest that their acts are religiously sanctioned.
mullah	Derived from an Arabic word meaning "master," and used as a title for Islamic religious leaders as well as local clerics in certain areas of the Muslim world. It is a common term for Shia clerics but is also used widely by Urdu-speaking Sunnis.

muqaddam	Arabic word meaning "assistant" or "facilitator." In this book, it refers to the starter kit used in teaching children to read the Qur'an.
Muslimah	Arabic feminine form of *Muslim*, denoting a Muslim girl or woman.
namaz	Persian and Urdu word for ritual prayer. See *salat*.
neo-Salafi	Term used to describe a renewed Islamic revivalist movement from the post-colonial era. This renewal is marked by strict literalist and puritanical interpretations of Islam. See also *Salafi*.
niat/niyat	Arabic word for "intention." In Islam, all acts of worship (prayer, fasting, charity, etc.) must be preceded by the individual believer's conscious intention in order to be valid.
nikah	Arabic word for the Islamic marriage contract.
ninety-nine names of God	Attributes found in the Qur'an and *sunnah* that describe the nature of God, such as omnipotent and merciful.
niqaab/niqab	Face veil usually leaving only the eyes exposed, traditionally worn by some Muslim women, especially on the Arabian Peninsula. Worldwide only a small minority of Muslim women wear *niqaab*, including a minority of those who consider themselves devout. Whether the wearing of *niqaab* is required, optional or undesirable has been a point of contention among competing interpretations of Islam. Differing views are put forth by those wishing to curb religious (especially Muslim) expressions of belief, those defending religious freedom, and those defending women's rights.
Peace be upon him.	Phrase written or spoken after the name of any prophet, as a way of showing honor and respect.
People of the book	Arabic: *Ahl al-kitab*. A Qur'anic term used to describe nations to whom God had

	revealed books before Muhammad, such as Jews, Christians, Sabians, and others. Some scholars believe that Zoroastrians, Hindus, and Buddhists are included in this group because they too have revealed scriptures.
pesa	Pakistani and Indian coin currency.
Prophet Muhammad	Muhammad ibn 'Abdullah, lived 570/571-632. Muslims believe that Muhammad was God's final messenger, who received the verses of the Qur'an, the literal word of God, over a period of twenty-two years up until his death. He is seen as the restorer of an uncorrupted original monotheistic faith going back to a line of prophets including Adam, Noah, Abraham, Moses, Jesus, and others. During his lifetime, Muhammad acted as religious, political, and military leader. Muslims consider Muhammad to have been the ideal Muslim and many seek to emulate his behavior in everyday life (see *sunnah*).
punishment of the grave	Refers to the suffering of the souls of the unrighteous in the grave during the time between death and the Day of Judgment.
purdah	From the Farsi (Persian) word for "curtain." *Purdah* refers to the cultural practice of gender segregation and modesty that dictates behavior among unrelated women and men in South Asian societies and includes various forms of covering of the female body.
Purim	Jewish festival commemorating the events recounted in the biblical book of Esther. It is a joyous celebration that includes the tradition of masquerading.
Qawwali	A form of Sufi devotional music popular in South Asia, with a tradition stretching back over 700 years. Nusrat Fateh Ali Khan was one of the most famous *Qawwali* singers.
Qur'an	Sacred scripture of Islam and primary source of Islamic law and theology. Muslims generally

	hold the Qur'an to be the literal word of God and His final revelation, gradually revealed to Prophet Muhammad from 610 to 632 CE.
rakat	One unit of Islamic ritual prayer (*salat*), which involves recitation of scripture and prayers while performing a complete sequence of physical postures including standing, kneeling and touching one's forehead to the ground. Each of the daily ritual prayers consists of several *rakats*.
Ramadan/Ramazan	The ninth month of the Islamic calendar, during which healthy, adult Muslims are expected to fast from dawn to dusk every day. This ritual fast is one of the five pillars of Islam. Its purpose is to foster introspection, self-discipline, and empathy with the poor and suffering, while strengthening community. The practice of fasting is learned socially and gradually and is not imposed on children. Fasting in Islam includes refraining from all food, drink, smoking, sexual activity, and resisting feelings of anger or ill will. Ramadan also is believed by Muslims to be the month during which the Qur'an was first revealed. It was considered a sacred month in pre-Islamic Arabia, as well.
tawhid	Arabic word meaning "unity, oneness." *Tawhid* is the core principle of Islam and refers to the oneness and indivisibility of God.
Salaam	Arabic word for "peace." *Salaam* is a common greeting among Muslims worldwide.
Salafi	Arabic term derived from the word "predecessors" or "forefathers," often referring to a school of Islamic revivalist thought that emphasizes the way of life of Prophet Muhammad's generation and rejects subsequent historical developments in Islamic thought. *Salafi* often is used synonymously with *Wahhabi*, including in this book, although it has multiple and varying definitions and usages.

salat	Ritual prayers performed by Muslims five times daily. *Salat* is the second of the five pillars of Islam.
SAWS	Abbreviation of *sala Allahu alaihi wa sallam*, an Arabic phrase meaning "May God honor him and grant him peace." Many Muslims say or write this phrase after the name of Prophet Muhammad.
shahada/shahadah	Arabic for "testimony [of faith]." The *shahada* is an Islamic statement of faith spoken when converting to Islam and frequently uttered in prayer and supplication. The *shahada* is also called the first pillar of Islam. "To take *shahada*" means to formally convert to Islam. See also *La illaha ill Allah wa Muhammad rasul Allah*.
Shalom aleikhem	Hebrew equivalent of the Muslim greeting *Salaam alaikum*, meaning "Peace be with you." Arabic and Hebrew are Semitic languages and have many words and grammatical features in common.
shari'a/shari'ah	Term referring to God's law or way of life for Muslims. Historically, Islamic scholars have generated the *shari'a* through extracting legally-oriented verses from the Qur'an and from legal pronouncements attributed to Prophet Muhammad. *Shari'a* is often mistranslated as Islamic law and mistaken to include *fiqh*, or Islamic jurisprudence, which is scholarly interpretation and expansion on *shari'a* principles.
shaykh/sheikh	Honorific title in Arabic for male elder. Muslim clerics are often referred to as *sheikh*. It is also the title for Sufi masters of a specific order.
Shia	Term used to refer to the largest minority sect within Islam. Shias make up about 15 percent of Muslims worldwide. However, they constitute the majority of Muslims in Iraq and the vast majority in Iran, where Shia Islam has been the official religion since the 16th century. Shia

	Islam first developed as a political movement after the death of Prophet Muhammad, but then developed some distinct theological teachings and religious practices.
shirk	Arabic word meaning "associating," specifically referring to associating other gods with Allah. This is an act or belief that violates belief in the unity or the oneness of God. It is often translated as "idolatry," but it encompasses more than that term suggests.
shura	Arabic word for "consultation" and used to mean "advisory council." Derived from tribal custom, it refers to a council composed of appointed or elected representatives.
Sufi	Somewhat generic term used to refer to the mystical branches, esoteric interpretations, special devotional practices, and orders of masters and initiates within Islam. Often Sufis are characterized as a "third sect" next to Sunnis and Shias. This is a misunderstanding, as the mystical path can be followed by Sunnis and Shias. In the West, Sufism is often taken to be the gentler or more inclusive brand of Islam. This characterization fails to take into account the wide diversity of interpretation and practice among Sufis, not all of whom engage in devotional singing or dance. It also does not take into account the diversity among Sunnis and Shias, who can be open-minded and spiritual without ascribing to mysticism.
sujud	Act of touching one's forehead to the ground in ritual prayer, signifying the worshiper's humility before and devotion to God.
sunnah	The comprehensive example of conduct and Islamic practices set by Prophet Muhammad, as recorded in his collected sayings (*hadith*) and his biographies. Traditionally, Muslims believe they are obliged to emulate the Prophet's *sunnah*. However, there are differences of opinion among Muslims as to how literally

	these examples are to be taken or which ones are more important than others. Thus, some might choose to emulate the Prophet's habits of hygiene while ignoring his compassionate and, in many ways, empowering treatment of women, or vice versa.
Sunni	Common term referring to the majority sect and legal schools within Islam. About 85 percent of the world's Muslims are Sunni. However, practices and beliefs among them vary according to local culture, legal school of interpretation, individual conscience, and other factors.
sura/surah	Chapter of the Qur'an. The Qur'an contains 114 *suras*.
SWT	Abbreviation of the Arabic phrase *Subhanahu wa ta'ala*, meaning "May He be glorified and exalted." This phrase is written or spoken by some Muslims after the name of God to express devotion.
tafseer	Genre of Qur'anic exegesis or scriptural interpretation.
tawhid	Arabic word for "unity," referring to the central Islamic concept of the oneness of God.
umrah	Arabic word referring to the voluntary pilgrimage to Mecca that can be undertaken at any time of the year (unlike *hajj* which takes place during certain days during *Dhul Hijjah*, the Islamic month of pilgrimage). *Umrah* includes some of the same rituals as *hajj* but is not identical to it and does not replace it.
ulema	Arabic word meaning "learned ones." The word is used to denote the educated class of Islamic legal scholars but can also refer to Islamic clergy of varying degrees of education.
Wahhabi	Revivalist movement of Islamic thought originating in Saudi Arabia in the 18th century, premised on the uncompromising unity of God and known for its strict interpretation

	of what constitutes *bid'a* (innovation), and its oppressive stance toward women and other Islamic sects, especially Shia and Sufi.
wau bulan	Malaysian moon-kite, made of colorful paper with floral motifs.
yarmulke	Cloth skullcap usually worn by Orthodox Jewish men at all times, and by some Conservative and Reform Jewish men during prayer.
zhikr/zikr	See *dhikr*.

CPSIA information can be obtained at www.ICGtesting.com
Printed in the USA
LVOW061522221211

260737LV00008B/25/P